Writing for Regional Publications

Writing for Regional Publications

Brian Vachon

Writer's Digest Books
Cincinnati, Ohio

Library of Congress Cataloging in Publication Data
Vachon, Brian, 1941-
    Writing for regional publications.
    Includes index.
    1. Authorship. 2. Journalism, Provincial—
United States. I. Title.
PN147.V23   808'.025'0973   79-9381
ISBN 0-911654-73-9

Book design by Barron Krody

Acknowledgments

Regional editors throughout the United States and Canada helped provide me with the information contained in this book and to them I am most grateful. My thanks also to Charlotte McCartney, Jean Snow, Janet Hubbard, Trudy Otis, Sally Willard, and to the editor of editors, Carol Cartaino. Special thanks, also, to Catherine Krupa.

Contents

Introduction
Writing for the Regionals

Introduction

Publishing has gone homegrown, I discovered a while ago. I could tell by my own reading habits and those of the people around me.

I began to notice the periodicals I spent time lingering over. And I began to make inquiries, first among acquaintances and then over a far wider spectrum.

I found us reading more about places and less about events. Looking for information about territory—the territory in which we reside, territory we would like to vacate to or vacation in, territory that by its very landscape, customs or people, day-to-day life or nightlife—territory that by its offer of excitement or relaxation, solitude or fellowship, intensity or space—meant something to us: that is what we are reading about these days.

You are witnessing a quiet revolution in publishing. The old publishing nerve centers—"New York, Chicago, Los Angeles—are losing their nerve. Places like Tucson and

Houston and Santa Barbara are taking it away. A spirit of localism is pulsing across the land. A magnificent opportunity for those of us who are looking for reading matter directly relevant to us; to what we know, are familiar with, want to know, want to be reminded of. The desire for more and better strictly provincial information is being fulfilled.

Just as surely as the old nerve centers (I've come to think of them as wind tunnels) are losing their monopoly on the printed word, so are they losing their importance as writers' havens, meccas, cities-of-opportunity.

There was a time not so long ago that a writer with no agent, no magazine connections, no family bankroll, no friends in publishing, and—in fact—nothing but talent, had to live in New York City. Or at least within commuting distance. New York was where the opportunities were: the big publishing houses and magazine conglomerates were all clustered there, swapping stories and dropping names and rehashing the same stale stories. A few writers with well-known names could hole up in Provincetown or San Francisco or Aspen or Chicago. But weren't they really telling the same stories in different accents?

Spot news, terror, protest, anger, rebuttal—that all has been nicely handled by national publications and continues to be.

But the new reader—you—wanted something more.

And the regionals began to happen—the city slicks with their in-depth investigations and off-beat timeliness; the county and state regional monthlies that promoted their places with a crusader's zeal; the weekly newspaper supplements that took time to smell the roses, or the lead paint, see the sunset for what it really is and local governing bodies for what they really are. The new regionals swelled the tide of old regionals who had long been suggesting that bad news isn't the only news that's fit to print.

Look at the publications not merely published in your region but based in your region. Some cover the business environment, other stick with the terrestrial environment. Some praise and other scrutinize. Some are stuffed in Sunday papers, some roll forth as books. Some are hot for handicrafts, honky-tonks, or history. But all are localized. They have staked their claim to some corner of this land, and are standing their ground with pride. For pride is what this fastest growing group of magazines is all about; pride in your place, be it Cuyahoga County, Cheyenne, Calgary or Cincinnati.

They all need writers—freelancers, if you'll dare call yourself that. They need them desperately. These popular and populist publications aren't looking for a long list of writing accomplishments. They are looking for a sense of wonder, perspective, or even awe. They are looking for fresh approaches and new ideas. The new writer—you—has something to offer.

Regionals are emerging as potentially the most lucrative and accessible market there is for people who like to earn money by putting words on paper. There has been a twenty-seven-fold increase in regionals in the past fifteen years, and new ones are appearing all the time.

This book is dedicated to the proposition that the bandwagon has plenty of room for you. The sooner you hop on, the longer the ride will be.

1

A Sense of Place

A roundup of regionals
and how they differ

Those who said the print media had seen better days spoke a little too soon. Everyone who said the future was in television and video didn't see the future unerringly. Magazines came back, and came back strong. Leading the way are the regionals. A new one is born, literally, every day. Every state already has at least one regional publication and most have many. Cities are spawning regionals with abandon. Sunday papers contain regional magazines. Counties are producing regionals and provinces and sections and *regions* are producing regionals. Private publishers are seeing that regionals make good business sense and governments are finding that regionals are ideal public relations aids. Everyone is getting into the regional publications act.

If you're a freelance writer and haven't cracked the regional writing market, you're missing a good bet. Someone else is writing an article that could have been written by you and someone else is getting paid for it. If you're a serious freelance writer, that doesn't make any sense at all. In the next chapter, I'll talk about why regional publishers need you. Right now, I'd like to talk about the regionals themselves. How did they get so popular?

They became popular because we made them that way. Those of us who are readers—and every good writer is an avid reader—have been turning more and more often to publications which reconfirm our sense of territorial security. A sense of place has become more and more important to us.

My place is Vermont. I live in a state that is coveted by millions of non-Vermonters and inhabited by only half a million new or legitimate Vermonters. (In this particular state, legitimacy means it takes more than one hand to trace back your Vermont generations.) When I see a publication about Vermont, my immediate reaction is to devour it, commit it to memory. The reason is simple: I've got a crush on my place. Reading about it confirms all my convictions about Vermont's innate superiority. When I read that Vermont is a progressive state, or a conservative state (I see no conflict with the two) or a rural or beautiful or unspoiled state, I say to myself, Ah hah! I was right. My place is indeed unique.

And folks who live in Twin Falls, Idaho; London, England; and La Jolla, California, feel that way about Vermont. *Vermont Life* magazine, the state's official quarterly, has subscribers in each of those places. (One of London's subscribers is Her Royal Majesty Queen Elizabeth, for reasons that escape me. But each year she renews her subscription.) It isn't necessary to reside in a place to feel some proprietary feelings for it. You can occupy a region or long for a region or be homesick for a region. It's still your place.

I subscribe to a regional called *New York*. It's a magazine that tells me about a region that used to be my place, and every once in a while—when I'm wishing Vermont had a Bloomingdale's or a Lincoln Center or a Madison Square

Garden—I miss that town. *New York* magazine keeps me in touch.

And I also subscribe to *Alaska* magazine. I've never been to that state—never even been close—and I don't know that I'd ever want to live there. But there's a part of me that does; a part of me that has a pioneer's instincts and a longing for a frontier to conquer. Alaska appeals to that adventurer in me.

Another regional that appears regularly in my Vermont mailbox is *Richmond* magazine. It brings springtime in the Blue Ridge Mountains, and the salty tang of sailing on Chesapeake Bay. Even though I am a "Yankee" (I did once live in the South) those warm breezes and soft seductive southern accents keep calling me home.

Regionals then, for their readers, perform at least three functions. They confirm my belief that my place is very special indeed. They comfort me when I think back, with tenderness, about a place that used to be mine. And they give me visions of greener pastures in a place that could be in my future.

No wonder regional magazines are so popular. They vary enormously in editorial content and style, but they all identify a region and devote themselves to it. Wise and successful freelance contributors get to know the form that devotion takes and how to please the editor with whom they are working.

It is to this end that prospective writers should be aware of the four distinct types of publications in the regional field.

First there are large city magazines (see Chapter 9). They include *New York, Washingtonian, Philadelphia, New West* and, curiously, *Texas Monthly.* The large city magazine doesn't necessarily confine itself only to the city, but covers its region like large city newspapers used to when magazines weren't around to compete and newspapers were at each others' throats for advertising revenue and exclusive stories. Large city magazines are tough. They brook no nonsense. They muckrake more than they pander. They'll give more bad reviews of restaurants, movies, plays and politics than good and if there is a controversy waiting around to be pounced upon, they will pounce.

Large city magazines can be published in small towns. Both the *Maine Times* and the *New Hampshire Times* fit practically all the criteria for a large city magazine except for their tabloid size, newsprint paper, and rural settings.

When a regional publication concentrates on crusades, negatives, investigations, exposes, evaluations, reviews, and political critiques, it's in the big city league. Don't waste the editors' time with garden-club announcements or scenic photo essays. The editors won't be interested.

On the other hand, make certain you know what is of interest. The *Valley Monthly: Magazine of the Greater Lehigh Valley* is an example of how a casual reader might get pointed in the wrong direction. The magazine is slick, printed on coated paper, full of color, and, at first glance, an apparent cheerleader for the good life in the Lehigh Valley. A second glance suggests otherwise. The contents of a recent issue included a report on alleged racism in Allentown, Pennsylvania's local government, an expose of the Valley's supposed pornography king, and the prediction that Valley theater groups are staging a losing comeback.

Westchester looks almost exactly like the *Valley Monthly* except for its logo, but it is one of the hundreds of new, positive regionals (see Chapter 8) where almost all the news is good and all the characters noble. *Westchester*, like *Valley News*, is privately owned and in business to make a profit. The fact that the contents of a typical issue are routinely optimistic ("Frugal Can Be Fun," "The Sport that Is Netting New Players: Squash Booms," and "Feed the Birds: A Colorful Action-packed Show Without Ever Having to Leave Your House") simply indicates that the owners of *Westchester* think suburban New York county's highly affluent residents are more interested in sanguine fare. The *Valley Monthly*'s Pennsylvania readers work largely in factories, on assembly lines, and hard. The publishers of that monthly believe their product will have its highest success if its contents are bold and challenging. Both groups are undoubtedly correct.

Privately owned regional monthlies abound but their grandparents in the positive publication field are state-owned monthlies and quarterlies that have been giving the good news for years, sometimes not always for a direct profit, but always with tourist dollars firmly in mind.

Vermont Life began in 1947 as a purely promotional vehicle. It became financially independent in 1970 but remains under state aegis.

Vermont Life's predecessor was a magazine called *Vermont Highways*, published in the early 1930s when highways were something Vermont was clearly without. The monthly talked a lot about road paving and gasoline tax (3.22 cents per gallon back in those days) and beautification projects. It was clearly imitating *Arizona Highways*, a colorful monthly that was attracting a lot of people to Arizona. Other regionals trace their roots back to local chamber of commerce printshops or mimeographed sheets that were handed to tourists at welcoming centers. Other regionals started big and got bigger. Young *Los Angeles* magazine sold more advertising pages than any consumer magazine in the country in 1978 and is still growing. *Beautiful British Columbia* and *North Dakota Horizons* are of the same ilk. The degree to which we promote our areas might differ, but we are all positive in our approach. ("Not unlike the overall effect of a pedigreed Irish Setter," a Vermont newspaper writer once wrote about *Vermont Life*. "Bred for good looks but lacking in brains or guts." He was wrong in that assessment, but not *dead* wrong. I let it go unchallenged.)

Positive regionals can be located in large cities. "Basically, we are committed to keeping our readers armed with helpful information that will enable them to enjoy and stay ahead in a rapidly changing, contemporary city," says the editor of *Richmond* (Virginia) magazine.

"We're interested in the news behind the news," says the

editor of *Baltimore* magazine, a monthly that is perhaps more positive than its editors would like to admit. "We want to tell why and how something happens, and we look for life-style articles that discuss what is going to happen rather than what has happened."

Positive publications might be state-owned, province-owned, county-owned, privately owned or sponsored by chambers of commerce or businessmen's groups. Some might be specifically pointed outside the region they represent—*Vermont Life* sends 90 percent of its subscriptions out of state—and others may be for local consumption. *Wonderful West Virginia* is aimed primarily at West Virginians. "The success of this magazine is state pride," says its editor, Ed Johnson. "We promote West Virginia." Inexpensively, I might add. When I asked Johnson what his range of payment was, he said "None. We do not have to pay."

Happily for freelancers, that attitude is rare—even in the most chauvinistic of regionals.

The highest payers are, predictably, the privately owned publications with the largest circulations.

"Back in 1935, *Yankee* magazine founder Robb Sagendorph wrote that 'Yankee's destiny is the expression and perhaps indirectly the preservation of that great culture in which every Yank was born and by which every real Yank must live.' *Yankee's* destiny has not changed in the over forty years since," says Judson D. Hale, the current editor. High-toned talk but well-deserved. Yankee is sent to 750,000 subscribers and pays up to $1,000 for feature articles.

Others in the high stratosphere economically include *Southern Living* for the South, the *Beaver* for eastern Canada, *National Geographic* for the planet, and *Omni* for the universe. It's a matter of defining your region.

A third genre of regional publication is the newspaper insert or Sunday supplement (see Chapter 10). This group enjoys the shortest lead time of any regional and therefore can come closest to actually covering an event. For weeklies like *New York*, press obligations make real timeliness almost impossible; but for a weekly like *Arizona*, the Sunday roto section of a number of Arizona newspapers, spot coverage and near news is possible.

Some Sunday inserts have the same aggressive desire to mix it up that city magazines display. "Almost nothing is holy and few things are worthy of solemn respect," says Editor Bud DeWald of *Arizona*. "Rarely is anything unique." (Tom Cooper, DeWald's counterpart at *Arizona Highways*, is the editor of a positive publication and takes a sharply contrasting point of view. His readers have an average age of 56, live mostly outside of Arizona, are affluent, travel-oriented, and close to retirement. "We want to provide a new means of showing Arizona to potential tourists, and articles which show the uniqueness of the state's attractions," he says. To him, there is much in Arizona that is holy and worthy of solemn respect.)

The fourth group of regional publications are guide and tour books, generally published annually, sometimes by private organizations, sometimes by public funds.

Guide and tour books, like positive publications, are unabashedly proud of the regions they want you to explore. Why would they exist if they felt otherwise? (Skeptics among you who suggest that privately published tour books just *might* exist to make money are probably on the right track. But let's not make a big thing of it here. Freelance contributors to tour guides should be thinking promotion, not profit.)

This group of publications generally operates with a long lead time, is strictly aimed at the regionally uneducated—visitors—and is filled with events listings, off-the-beaten-path attractions, on-the-beaten-path attractions, and any-thing else that will make the tourist enjoy his stay and want to come back again next year.

The final group of regionals, and perhaps the group most marginally self-sufficient (if they are at all) are the environmental magazines. They are concerned with saving natural areas, endangered species, public land, and their region's sense of place. Often sponsored or underwritten by natural resource foundations, environmental societies, or state environmental agencies, they sing the song of the great outdoors and their contributors had better know the tune. Clean water, housing developments, cutting ski trails, all-terrain vehicles that do the least environmental damage, dams, proposed state or federal legislation all get serious treatment in these publications. There is precious little humor and—more than any other group of regional magazine—facts and figures take precedence over style. But being serious doesn't have to mean sedentary, and the best of the environmental magazines can be as pleasing as they are informative.

In this list of regional publications, there are areas of obvious overlap. Some positive publications get mighty environmentally aware at times and some city magazines occasionally take on the accent of a city guide and tour book. Some newspaper inserts you'll see are so slick they could sell very nicely on their own. The lines of separation blur and the categories become fuzzy.

But so what? No publication is like any other, and that's what makes the current regional magazine explosion so exciting. There are so many magazines out these days, and they all have to be written. Regional publications share that one, crucial commonality. They have to be written. Someone has to put words into sentences and paragraphs that make up stories which, with a bit of luck, a lot of intelligent scouting and diligent writing, get accepted. And paid for!

Regionals are a kind of publication, and their timeliness has never been more on target. For the first time in decades, newspapers and the national media (with its penchant for bad news) left the door open for stories of a more provincial nature. And people want to read something besides guerilla warefare accounts and muggers' arrests. They want to read about home, and they want to read good news.

The difference among the countless regionals is a difference in readership. Examine all publications closely before submitting. Writers who have a high placement ratio of story ideas have learned what editors are looking for and supply just that. It's this kind of research that separates would-be writers from successful ones.

Target the reader, and you will know what the editor of a regional is looking for. Are they blue-collar workers in Philadelphia? Then *Philadelphia* magazine is looking for hard-hitting accounts that make readers sit up and take notice.

Are they city dwellers who look to Vermont as an oasis of sanity and beauty? Then *Vermont Life*, the magazine I edit, looks for articles which confirm that belief. Our articles say "Yes, it's still here, and it's still pretty much the way it used to be. Oh, there are a few more cars and not as many small farms, but it's still pretty much the way you remember it."

Look for the subtleties in the tone of voice in a magazine and you will have mastered one of the major tricks of freelance writing. If the tone is harsh, write harsh. If it is serene, write serene. Remember, no editor of anything—especially regional publications—is going to change magazine policy to fit your editorial style. That's just simply never done. You have to adjust to us. It's the first Rule of the Writer's Jungle. "Give the editor what he wants because ultimately, he will get it from someone and it might as well be you." (I add, in the protection of parenthesis, that I don't at all mean editors are looking for identical *styles* in the writing we accept. We take great pleasure in seeing a multitude of styles, and personal flairs and individual touches. But we can't have variety in policy. *Vermont Life* doesn't publish stories about trailer parks. If there is something called the *Trailer Park News*, and I suspect there must be, I'm sure it never published stories about Vermont farmhouses.)

The Second Rule of the Writer's Jungle says: "Keep looking. If it's a good idea, somebody's going to buy it." The third and final rule says: "Do it!"

Freelancers Wanted

No experience necessary

Vermont Life magazine has been called the state's number one public-relations tool. Over 100,000 copies are sent each quarter to avid readers and viewers whose subscription renewal rate is consistently over 80 percent. (That's why I called them avid. *Time* or *Newsweek* would be delighted with a return of 50 percent.) It's a magazine with an international reputation, established many years before I arrived, and one which will be retained many years after I leave.

I am the editor of *Vermont Life*. I've been associated with many other magazines—*Psychology Today*, *Newsweek*, *Saturday Review* among them—but this is the magazine that I've enjoyed helping select and shape the contents of best. This one is a delight because, as is the case in most regional publications, its purpose is purely to give pleasure.

I am also the only staff writer at *Vermont Life*. I once talked our managing editor into writing a piece for us. We had received some charming photographs of sheets and pillowcases hanging to dry on a farmhouse porch right after a sudden freeze. Linda Paradee said she remembered when those freezes sometimes happened to her mother in late fall. The sheets and pillowcases would be stiff as boards, and they'd crackle if you tried to fold them. She wrote about her memories, and those words accompanied the photographs most agreeably.

But in recent years, that has been the extent of staff help in writing. I do a column each issue, provide words for our quarterly scenic section, write advertising copy, do all the captions, the table of contents, an occasional introduction of contributors, and the titles and subtitles. That's about as much writing as I really want to do each issue, but once in a while I also provide an article. (Since I can't pay myself for writing for *Vermont Life*, I'm my own most inexpensive author and when our budget is a little tight, I give myself assignments.)

So at the very maximum, I provide 10 percent of the words that go into every issue of the magazine. The remaining 90 percent—or about eighty articles a year—come from the outside, from freelance writers. Some come as direct assignments from me, some come after I've expressed interest in a written query, some even come over the transom. But they all come from the outside, mostly from writers who are also housewives or architects or teachers or whatever. There aren't many full-time writers in these parts. For my money, there aren't enough part-time writers either. I'm always on the lookout for new talent.

But I wondered if I were the only editor of a regional magazine who was constantly on the lookout for competent writers. Do my counterparts in city, county, and provincial magazines throughout this part of the world also worry about finding a steady supply of stylish, original, intelligent prose? Were their staffs as small and needs as great?

I decided to take a survey. Shamefully exploiting my position as president of the Regional Publishers' Association (a position I was elected to when the association members decided Vermont would be a good place to hold their annual meeting), I polled all the editors in the United States and Canada who were members in good standing. Then I polled all the editors who were not members in good standing. Then I polled the editors of every city, state, county, sectional, and provincial magazine I could track down, using *Writer's Market*, the *Readers' Guide to Periodic Literature*, and *Literary Market Place* as my sources.

The appeal I made was fairly straightforward. I sent all these editors a personalized letter, asking for their help and information. I enclosed a questionnaire, thanked them in advance for answering it, tucked a stamped, self-addressed envelope into each package, and sent them off. Hundreds of them.

Regional magazine editors turned out to be very obliging folks. Hundreds of completed questionnaires were returned to me. And the answers I received confirmed the fact that I am not at all a rare species of editor, depending—as greatly as I do—on outside help.

Asking, "What percentage of your material comes from freelancers?" something called the *Oregon Voter Digest* with a circulation of 3,000 replied "minimal" and something called *Sunset* with a circulation of 4 million said "none." The rest of the editors were somewhat more encouraging.

Daniel Malkovich, editor and publisher of *Illinois* magazine, who said his editorial staff was as minuscule as mine, said *all* his material was from freelance writers. Ann Lewis, who has made *Georgia Life* a beacon of literary light in her state for years, wrote: "Probably one-third of our manuscripts come unsolicited. Our 'regular contributors' are also freelance writers which would mean practically all the contents are freelance-written. We've never had a staff writer."

After that the percentages started dropping, but not very fast and not very far. Most regional publication editors confirmed what I half-suspected. Ninety percent of the material they publish comes from outside the house. *Chicago*

Reader, with an editorial staff of seven and a circulation of nearly 100,000, gets 80 percent from freelancers. *New York* magazine with an editorial staff of forty gets half its material from freelancers.

My survey of regional publication editors told me that we had other things in common besides small staffs and a heavy dependence on freelancers.

The results showed that the overwhelming number of editors prefer written queries. They shy away from long, nostalgic tales. They generally eschew poetry, politics, and "very, very short articles," which—says the editor of *Nebraskaland* magazine—"are usually the poorest quality." Fiction is largely unpopular. Except for the more sophisticated city magazines, restaurant and movie reviews don't elicit much excitement.

But what do regional editors like least? Virtually every editor I polled gave some version of the same answer, but James D. Selk, editor of *Madison* magazine in Wisconsin, stated it with delicate simplicity.

"What sort of articles are you most interested in?" I asked in my questionnaire.

"Pieces with a strong Madison angle," he responded.

"What articles get almost automatic rejection slips?"

"Anything without a strong Madison angle."

In this vein, A.D. Hopkins, editor of the *Nevadan*, says, "We are not kidding about the regional angle. Though most writers seem to ignore it. It is required, period."

If any writer ever asked me what the best market for his or her material was *anywhere*, I'd say look to your regional. No matter where you live, you've probably got one covering your area and more likely, you have a dozen. There are twelve publications that cover Vermont besides *Vermont Life*. *Yankee* magazine, and *Blair & Ketchum's Country Journal*—who don't relish being mentioned in the same sentence—cover New England (though the latter is expanding its region to make it national in scope). Four Vermont newspapers have special Sunday inserts that cover parts of the state. There are environmental magazines that inspect Vermont and annual guides that give the wheres and the whens. A Vermont literary magazine will surface now and then, as will Vermont underground "newspapers" (which are much more regional publications than they are purveyors of news). Anyone who has a good Vermont story and the ability to write it should be published and paid within a year. That also goes for a good Alaska, Florida, Nebraska, Alabama, Regina, Philadelphia, or Wichita story. The market is wide open.

"What I like to do is get to know a few reliable freelancers, who are willing to work for low pay, and assign stories to them," says the editor of *Trenton* magazine, a business-oriented New Jersey monthly. But by "low pay" she means $25 to $75 for short articles, and while that's on the thin end as regionals go, it's certainly not highway robbery. Any writer who has ever tried to buy a week's worth of groceries with the check from a poetry magazine, library science journal, or, heaven forbid, a religious periodical would find *Trenton* checks very satisfying.

Charles Turney Stevens, editor of *Nashville!* says his contributors must be local people because of the particularly parochial nature of his publication. I don't question his editorial policy. But I'll bet I could get published in *Nashville!* next year, under an assumed name, without ever leaving my home town of Montpelier.

You *do* have to know a region to write about it, but you don't necessarily have to live there. I know Nashville pretty well — used to cover the Tennessee legislature there when I was a newspaper reporter. I know the people to call who would give me the people to get in touch with to put a good lively *Nashville!* story together.

On the other hand, I can't say the same thing about a magazine called *Glimpses of Micronesia & the Western Pacific.* Though they pay 10 cents a word, which is certainly okay, and though they want articles that are lively and factual, which I think I'm capable of, that's a publication whose half-million readers will never see my words. I don't know where Micronesia is, for one thing. For another, I think of the Pacific as already west and so, in my limited geographical perceptions, the *western* Pacific would be smack in the Far East. I don't know anyone there to call, and wouldn't if I did. Or at least I would not want to call until after five or on weekends. But when do they have weekends in the western Pacific?

I will labor the point no further. You can't write about what you don't know about, and that's a fact. You *can* research an area without actually residing in it, and that's another fact. *Vermont Life* never publishes photographs taken outside Vermont's borders, but the magazine's two most active photographers live in New York and Washington, D.C. We've had articles published by authors who make their homes in Pittsburgh, Pennsylvania; Berkeley, California; and Corpus Christi, Texas, among other exotic spots. The authors had only one thing in common: they knew Vermont.

The regional market is wider than the region you happen to call home. And it is one market where enthusiasm will help open doors. When a writer sends a query to the editor of *Oklahoma Today* and lets it be known that Will Rogers has always been his hero or that Tulsa is his kind of town, the editor will know he's hearing from his kind of writer. Editors like to see evidence of regional pride in their writers—even editors of the tough-talking city magazines. "We think of ourselves as 'proudly provincial'" says Richard L. Hirsch, editor of *BFLO* of Buffalo, New York, "even though we look at our community with a somewhat irreverent, opinionated attitude."

One of the delights of working with any regional is that the writing gives you a chance to brag a little about the region you're writing about. You get to share some enthusiasm, feed some fantasies, confirm some exciting suspicions. Regional magazines work on the pleasure principle, except for the most cynical urban slicks (and even the editor of consciously caustic *New York* gets upset when people take snipes at the

Big Apple). Writers in our market are people who know how to make other people feel good about a place. That's a very special kind of writing and not particularly the kind that can be churned out in volume by the self-styled professionals. Freelancers new to the profession might have the kind of fresh ideas and unaffected style regional editors are looking for.

I once looked down a *Vermont Life* table of contents and realized, with some surprise, that half the articles in that issue were written by people who were seeing their by-line for the first time. It wasn't planned that way but that's the way it happened. One of those writers was 23 and fresh out of graduate school. Another was 95 and had been a farmer in Thetford, Vermont, for all of this century.

When I asked other regional editors if they dealt much with newcomers to the writing field, the unanimous answer was yes. "The fellow who bangs out words all day to make a living isn't likely to catch our readers' fancy about New England," says *Yankee* managing editor John Pierce. "We're looking for unique approaches, and often those come from new writers."

Regionals are also ideal for freelancers because they offer such diversity. Vermont, third smallest state in the union, could keep me busy assigning story ideas if *Vermont Life* were a weekly. And you could drop Vermont into most states and all Canadian provinces and lose it. I worry about the editors of specialty magazines: aren't they eventually going to run out of things to write about sailboats, or horses, or skateboards, or motor homes? Won't the last true confession soon be told? Won't *Glamour* eventually run out of ways to tell women how they can be more coquettish and *Ms.* come up dry on ways to tell women how to be more assertive? But regionals never run out of things to say because the region never stays the same. If *Philadelphia* ran one profile a month on an interesting Philadelphian, it would be well into the next century before it made a dent in the current batch of brotherly lovers. *Adirondack Life* switched from quarterly to bimonthly simply because there was so much to say about that particular region. And from my side of Lake Champlain, the Adirondacks look like one big tedious forest.

Some magazines exist to be irreverent. "Almost nothing is holy and few things are worthy of solemn respect" says the advise to writers handed out by *Arizona* magazine. "Rarely is anything unique."

Other magazines are unabashedly chauvanistic. (It's such a pleasure to use that word correctly.) "We cover Texas, boy," says Frank Lively, editor of *Texas Highways*, addressing writers of both genders, "and that's a good chunk of real estate. Our readers like historical articles about old forts, cowboys, trails, longhorns, buffalo. We give 'em plenty of Texas sort of things."

Still others are in business to make money. To suggest their purpose was anything more than the bottom line would be stretching the truth, but to keep that bottom line in the black, most privately owned publications are edited for sure sales. "We try to be unpredictable," says *Washingtonian* editor John Limpert. "We have no formula. We publish some investigative material, some service material, some nostalgia, some psychological-sociological articles, some profiles of people, some profiles of institutions. We try to avoid covering the same ground that newspapers cover."

Regionals are personal, and that's what makes this particular market so satisfying for writers *and* editors. I have a sign on my wall that says "Take a Writer to Lunch" and I obey it frequently. I want to get to know the people who are potential contributors. Regional editors aren't interested in talking with your agent. They want to know you. We can't afford to be impersonal with our contributors. We have to get to know you, and rely on you (we have no research staff to test reliability, remember), and know that you will be future sources of good copy. The regional market is wide open to freelancers and so are regional publication editors. We *want* writers to ask us questions, and we enjoy answering them. In the end, that saves us headaches, broken deadlines, irritated press operators and discontented subscribers. Who needs any of that?

Regional publications present ideal markets to freelance writers because we *need* them. Make them you. You'll find yourself in mighty good company.

3

Little Things Mean a Lot

How to turn an editor off

I spent one year of my life—my 29th, to be exact—doing something a great many writers think about, wonder and worry about, and hope to do one day. I spent that year as a freelance writer. Period. No other means of support. No sidelines or rich relatives. Just me, living in New York City, bursting with what I considered good ideas and hoping to develop some good connections.

The decision to spend some time solely as a freelance writer was not difficult to make. The magazine which I had previously been editing was aimed at teenagers. Some of the things we accomplished were damned remarkable: interviews with Elton John, Melanie, Linda Ronstadt, and Masters and Johnson, all before most people had ever heard of those luminaries. That was the problem. We weren't merely ahead of our time. We were light-years away. As a result, teenagers failed to buy the magazine in huge numbers. My paychecks began to bounce and my publisher stopped showing up at the office. I saw the handwriting on the wall and quit.

I quickly got some assignments from *Look* magazine, where my father had been employed as a photographer for twenty years; sold a piece on late-night television movies to *Playboy*; and signed a contract with a book publisher to write about the Jesus Movement in California in the early 1970s. I was on my way. What the hell. A steady job was an inconvenience; a regular paycheck a stale custom. I was single and money was coming in, in very agreeable lumps. Full-time freelancing was going to be the life for me. I had it made.

For about two months. Then it started to unravel a little. I had to sit down and actually write the book I had contracted to do. Moreover, I had to come up with some additional magazine or book ideas. My cash input began to dwindle, and it seemed like my creative imagination was dwindling at an equal rate. I quickly slipped past nervous into panic. I was getting phone calls of the wrong kind.

If you've never been called by a professional dunner (that character paid to collect delinquent debts), you'll be unable to fully share this experience. I can't describe the telephone voice of a dunner, and I can't imitate it. I can only say, when you pick up a ringing phone and hear your name rasped in an unmistakably menacing tone that efficiently packs genuine evil, you *know* you've been addressed by a dunner. You know immediately that some check bounced or some bill was overdue or ignored, and you also know that unless you hang up, you're going to be stuck apologizing to someone who doesn't know you or care about your excuses. He simply wants your money. Generally, he's not a nice person, and that gets conveyed very quickly.

Dunners never failed to mispronounce my last name. It was always, "Brian Vaccone?" In truth, my last name has a shhh in it, as in "sherbert" (or, to be more apt, "sheriff"). But for reasons that strike me as being eerily coincidental, the various dunners assigned to my various cases were unable to pronounce my name correctly. They all said "Vaccone."

To this day, when someone makes that mistake with my last name, I get a cold sweat. Needless to say, when a freelance, would-be contributor to a magazine I'm editing makes that mistake I am unconsciously but absolutely set in a negative frame of mind. If, for example, Jerome David Salinger offered to write a piece for *Vermont Life* about what it was like sitting on his porch outside Lyme, New Hampshire, looking across the river to the green hills of Vermont, and mispronounced my name while making the offer, I'd turn him down.

Now that I've told you the background, you can understand why I don't like to hear my name mispronounced. Or, for that matter, misspelled. That turns me off. And if you are trying to appeal to my editorial instincts and possibly get an assignment from me, the last thing you want to do is turn me off. You'll want to start by getting my name right. And my title. I'm the editor, not the *managing* editor. Try for my correct address and zip code, too. By whatever means, get this information straight.

(Since this chapter began autobiographically to make my opening point, I'll quickly close the story with a parenthetical update. To wit: I made lots of money the year I was a freelance writer. I spent lots more than I made. After that year, I went to work for *Saturday Review* and married a wonderful woman who is a certified public accountant. We never get dunning calls. And I don't think I'll ever be a full-time freelance writer again.)

Everyone tells you that editors are human and most of my personal experiences lead me to believe that's true. Editors of regional magazines may be a little more human than most. Our skin is a little thinner than editors of, say, skiing magazines, news magazines, or movie gossip magazines. The thin skin has several causes.

For one thing, we're not very well known. We're near the top of our profession, but we're not celebrities. In fact we don't come close. We're never asked to be guests on "Hollywood Squares" or panelists on "Meet the Press."

We're seldom even interviewed by our local newspapers. But we're *editors*. Ours is almost always the first name on the masthead and practically everyone doesn't know us.

Quick, give me the names of three regional magazine editors.

I didn't think you could. And yet those of us who became editors of regional magazines traveled a long way in our professions to land the jobs we have now. If we had put the same time and talent and upward mobility into politics, for example, we'd be high elected officials today. If we put that energy into the priesthood, we'd most surely be bishops.

But we're editors. And practically no one knows who we are; people don't know our names, not to mention our faces. So when you learn the name of an editor of a regional magazine, don't mispronounce it. He or she is thin-skinned.

We are sensitive for another reason. There is a segment of the population in the region we're presenting which doesn't want our magazine to exist. We share the distinction of being the only group of magazines on earth, with the exception of hardcore pornography magazines, that has people who would like to see us permanently out of business. Why? Because those people think we're doing our job too well. The editor of *Arizona Highways* shouldn't show all those gorgeous pictures of the Grand Canyon, the greasewood shrub and Mogollon Rim volcano. There are always enough people in Arizona. Same goes for Sante Fe, Bucks County, Manitoba, and every other region. "Don't make Vermont seem so damned attractive," a small but vocal minority tells me on a regular basis. "You're going to lure more flatlanders up here. And we've got plenty of them already."

So regional editors are always a little on guard, a bit defensive. And they also are straddling a helluva fence, or, as we say in Vermont, they're "between a rock and a hard place." They invariably love the region they are extolling (or exposing) and they realize there's a little bit of truth in the accusations of the opposition. Take me for example. I have tender feelings for this place called Vermont. Wouldn't want to live in any other spot on this earth. And I *definitely* think Vermont has too many flatlanders living here, bringing city ways and toying with Vermont traditions. The gates should have been shut just after I was permitted to enter the state. I should have been the last flatlander allowed in.

Yet I edit a magazine that makes Vermont look mighty appealing, which it is, and I'm positive that my magazine has influenced some New Jersey family to move up here and build a monstrous, ugly prefabricated townhouse on the side of a previously untouched green mountain. The editor of *New Jersey* knows surely that because of his fine magazine, some family of Vermont woodchucks (a derogatory name for honest Vermonters) moved into his state and got jobs that would have otherwise been given to honest New Jerseyites. Oregon doesn't have a state magazine because former governor, Tom McCall, was afraid his state would lose its identity through influx of outsiders. Florida on the other hand has spawned dozens of regional publications.

So you see, we've got our problems. First, we have anonymity. Second, we have enemies. And third, we know our enemies are partly right. There is an argument that says our publications shouldn't exist, and it is sometimes difficult to come up with a particularly salient counter-argument. We say we're good for tourism, which is true, and that we appeal to people outside the region who used to live inside and who are homesick. That's also true. We say we present a way of life that is unique and that should be documented. That's especially true.

But there's still that prefab townhouse on the side of that green mountain. So understand us regional editors. Be sensitive with us. Know about our problems.

Also, know about our *regions*. I'm continually amazed at how many letters I receive which begin with these words: "While I've never actually visited Vermont, I feel like I know it well enough to write an article for you." Talk about letters that never get finished. . .those letters don't even get preprinted responses. They go directly to the round-out box, only to be "considered" one last time by the maintenance technicians.

Knowing a region doesn't necessarily mean you have to live there. But you do have to have more than an abstract image or whimsical view of the territory and its inhabitants. Writers turn regional editors off when they advertise their ignorance. If you were the editor of *Gourmet* magazine, what would you think of a query that began like this: "I realize I'm no expert on wine. If the truth were known, I can hardly tell a Baron de Rothschild Savignon '39 from Gallo Hardy Burgundy. But let me tell you about a little vineyard I drove by the other day which I think really might make an interesting. . . ." Of course you'd throw that query away. The writer was practically begging you to. Or how about this for starters: "I may not know how refrigerators make water freeze, but I can tell you a great deal about ice." How would that sit with the editor of *Popular Mechanics*?

Regional magazines are the *Gourmets* of their domains. Their editors like style and verve and punch and query letters but they are totally deterred by territorial illiteracy. When writing for a regional it's essential to know the territory, its people and the characteristic qualities that make them special.

"Articles that don't have a regional angle (despite the fact that it was made very clear in *Writer's Market* that the magazine insists on a regional angle) get automatic rejection slips," says the editor of the *Las Vegas Review-Journal Nevadan*. "That mistake is the writer's fault and not the magazine's. We find it *extremely* irritating."

Does that sound like a turned-off editor? You bet it does. How about a query which begins like this?

What is *Vermont Life*'s policy regarding unsolicited articles? I have an article, including some excellent photographs, of some peregrine falcons in southern Vermont. The article reflects *Vermont Life*'s general theme and I would like to submit it for publication.

That poor would-be writer made four major mistakes in the first paragraph of her query. She may have made more mistakes later but I didn't see them because I didn't read the rest of the letter. The opening paragraph withered the possibility of any further interest.

What were the mistakes? To begin with, she was asking me about my magazine's policy. An unfortunate question asked by people unlikely to be published in *Vermont Life*. If you want to find out about a magazine's policy, you either study a few back issues and try to figure it out or you buy a current *Writer's Market* and have it succinctly explained. Beginning a letter with an unneccesary inquiry is a weak introduction which encourages a direct path to the wastebasket.

Her second mistake was to tell me she already had the article completed and ready to ship. When a writer tells me that, I am immediately put off. The writer is telling me that she has written something that might be right for me without asking my advice first. The writer has gone ahead without taking advantage of any wisdom I might have been able to pass along to her. Remember, I'm sensitive. I'm an editor of a regional and I overreact to people who take my skills lightly.

The third mistake was that she obviously didn't know we had published a short article on the peregrine falcon in a very recent issue. The writer was telling me that she didn't read my magazine very often or very closely. That hurt my feelings.

Finally, the writer referred to *Vermont Life*'s "general theme." I don't know that we have a general theme. We have a general territory—Vermont—but theme? Absolutely not. We have sad stories and funny stories and nostalgic stories and nature stories and human stories, but we don't have general theme stories.

That query did have one positive aspect. The writer said she had some "excellent photographs." There is nothing wrong with a touch of self-promotion. If you have some photographs you think are excellent, share that thought with the editor you are querying. He won't mind reading that at all. Or if you've recently published something in a national magazine, somehow let that fact slip out. If you went to prep school with the editor's daughter, go ahead and tell him. It won't hurt, and it somehow may work positively on the fellow's fragile psyche. Self-promotion, when it is gentle and calm, does writers all sorts of good.

But the self-promotion was the only good thing the Falcon Lady had to offer—one positive and four negatives—and in query letters, four into one won't go.

How about this query I received recently?

Thanks to Edison, the Wright Brothers, Henry Ford, Edwin Land and hundreds of other inventors, American factory hands have long been the most productive workers in the industrial world.

For one thing, that's not true. Japanese factory workers are generally more productive than their American counterparts. Prospective writers should make darn sure to get their facts straight.

Also, what on earth does any of that have to do with Vermont—my region, the most rural state in all of America? But something got to me about that letter. In some bizarre and masochistic manner, my curiosity was aroused. So I read on.

And on. And in the sixth paragraph, I finally found something that vaguely concerned Vermont. It was a mention of a business consulting firm in Durham, New Hampshire.

That did it. The letter got an automatic rejection and I went on to the rest of my mail but in a slightly disgruntled frame of mind. A would-be writer had made me wade through six puffy, generalized, unorganized paragraphs and then told me that the story he hoped to sell was headquartered in New Hampshire. An approach like that just doesn't make any sense. It's like telling the manager of McDonald's that you just savored the most wonderfully luscious hamburger. . .down the road at Burger King.

As I was throwing that letter away, I noticed that it had

been dictated. I saw the reference symbols "RH:dm" on the lower left-hand corner of the page and realized that the man who had offended me for six paragraphs had dictated his query to a secretary. It was "dm" who had actually written the letter. "RH" had only spoken some words. In fact, there was a darned good chance he didn't even do *that*. Probably "dm" did the creating at "RH' "s direction. And I figure if "RH" was the kind of person who would let his secretary do his querying for him, he's not my kind of writer.

Maybe that's because I've never learned how to dictate and am slightly envious of people who have. In any case, I'd rather hear directly from the secretary.

Letters that start off with "Dear Sir" turn me off and letters that start off with "Dear Gentleperson" make me worry seriously about my most recently ingested meal.

On the other hand, I don't like people who address me as "Dear Brian" when they don't know me. That's a little bit more familiarity than I can be comfortable with. (Remember, regional editors are touchy about rather mundane things.) I personally have long ago dispensed with the use of any conventional title of courtesy except when addressing a woman who is seventy or older, never been married and of some wealth. I will call her "Miss." All other prefixes are wasted syllables in my book, and so "Dear Brian Vachon" works best with me. If you're not sure what works best for the editor you're about to query, call and ask his or her secretary. A simple telephone call like that might mean the difference between a rejection and an assignment.

I get turned off by people who scold me in their query letters. One writer wrote me about doing a piece on the Vermont Symphony, and I replied that the idea did not fill me with anticipation and joy because arts articles generally didn't work in a magazine like *Vermont Life*. The would-be author was persistent and wrote me another letter; the last two sentences went like this: "As for your confessed bias against arts articles, I think you should be aware that the arts are on the rise in Vermont and potentially a good source of tourist activity. I hope you can use the article." Well, I couldn't. He made absolutely certain of that.

I am not the only editor who is occasionally admonished by a query letter. The editor of *Yankee* magazine is periodically asked why he doesn't feature articles on New England's discotheques. (This is to the editor of a publication with a traditional, colonial nature.)

When the editor of *Missouri Life* is told that he has failed to deal seriously with the poor elevator service in many St. Louis department stores, he will move on ever-so-quickly to his next piece of mail.

Editors of regional magazines also stay as far away as possible from writers who are condescending toward the inhabitants of the region. Virtually every attempt at reproducing a dialect is condescending—no matter how unintentional—and editors don't like it.

> Mah people come hyar a hunnert yars ago, 'n built up that thyar cabbun. Thay thought this hyar wuz about thuh purtiest thang they ever saw. They ain't never seen nuthin' purtier. But yew cain't dew nuthin' with it. Won't grow nuthin'. Mah Aint Betsy used to grow taters up aroun' thuh outhouse, but thuh county agint tole us not to grow nuthin' roun thar no more. Don't make no sense. Damn city folk. Got no use fer 'em.

That was an abortive and condescending attempt at reproducing the speech of Ozark hill people. It simply doesn't work.

I got a letter from someone who introduced himself pleasantly enough as a young freelancer, new to the area, who wanted to write about contra dancing, an art form and recreation that is indigenous to this region. I read his query with some interest until I got to this sentence: "A contra dance is usually an extremely informal affair with blue jeans considered fancy and Gatorade mixed with vodka considered the normal drink."

That turned me off. That told me the writer thought he was somehow superior to people who enjoy contra dancing. He viewed them as objects of some scorn, though if I had confronted him with that deduction, he would have heatedly denied it. But it was nonetheless true. You don't write that "Gatorade mixed with vodka is considered the normal drink" about people you respect and admire. Do you think *Texas Highways* would sport descriptions of "swaggering cowboys decked in ten-gallon hats?" And I wouldn't suggest slipping Polish jokes in an article intended for *Wisconsin Trails*. I hope I've made my point.

Here's another turn-off that appeared in my mail recently:

Dear Sir or Madame:
 I am a young freelancer who has been published in various regional magazines. I would like to propose an article that I feel would be interesting to readers of *Vermont Life*.

If you remember that I have an editorial staff of one and that I receive dozens of article queries a day, you'll understand why that opening paragraph turned me off. Not only did the writer not bother to determine my gender, much less my name, but I was also compelled to read a thirty-two word paragraph that told me nothing. I could have spent those seconds more productively by loosening my tie, or taking off my shoes.

She did not enhance her purpose in any way and succeeded in stifling any further interest on my part. This often happens to editors like me who find that there are just not enough hours in a day. My time is precious. So, future inquirers, get to the point. Make that first paragraph exciting. Make me want to read on.

(It turned out she wanted to write an article about how small investors can buy gold, and I'm sure—though the letter was not a copy—identical versions went to regional editors all over the hemisphere. Multiple querying may or may not be moral—I personally think it is not—but multiple querying to a regional editor on a subject that has nothing to do with the region is a good way to stay out of the profit end of the writing business.)

I'm turned off by proposals of stories about Vermonters who went somewhere else and made good. My friend Judson

Hale at *Yankee* says he's turned off by articles "written in the first person by a cat, dog or other animal." He also automatically rejects anything that is pornographic, deals with drugs, alcohol, or contains excessive profanity. That probably holds true for most regional editors—with the city magazine folks a notable exception.

Harry Hope of *Sandlapper* in South Carolina has a quick pink slip for "essays on Southern life inspired by *Mandingo* or *Li'l Abner*." He also says he's not likely to think kindly on anything that centers around grits or peanuts. Like the rest of us, he's heard all the clichés about his region and is bored by them. Believe me, query letters highlighting the subject of covered bridges or "My Wonderful Weekend in Vermont" are not apt to receive even a Vermont "a-yuh" as a go ahead in my regional magazine. I'm also sure that the editor of *Alaska* would like to have seen his last "how-to-construct-an-igloo" story. (Although an inventive writer might be able to breathe new interest into the topic by describing an economically feasible way to construct an igloo out of plastic.) The editor of *New Hampshire Profiles*, on the other hand, might be very interested in an article on conventional iceblock homes.

Regional editors, as a group, don't like a lot of footnoting in articles. Anything that looks like it might have been a doctoral thesis gets an unenthusiastic reception.

We also can't stand the "I used to live in your area" or "I just moved into your city" or "last autumn, the little woman and I drove through your lovely state" stories. Handwritten articles, queries on postcards, queries that are obviously contrived to fit the region ("The Machine Tool Industry Lives in Montana," "Alabama's Snowmobile Country," "Urban Pressures and the Saskatchewan Housewife," "Chicago's Covered Bridges"), anything not double-spaced, well-worn aspects of local history ("We still get about three a year on the midnight ride of Paul Revere," says the editor of the *New England Guild*), nonsensical pieces, blatant business promotions, and unsolicited articles are generally greeted unkindly by regional editors.

Phone queries turn off 98 percent of the would-be recipients. If in doubt, type.

Factual errors infuriate regional editors. If they catch one in a manuscript, they'll know you didn't research intelligently and they'll send you packing. But far worse is the factual error the editor doesn't catch. There is nothing that can more thoroughly unmake my day than to be told that the man identified as John Smith on page sixteen is really his brother Harry or that when we gave the population of Vershire, Vermont, at 360, we were off by seventy-two folks. Do that to me dear writer, and I not only won't accept your apology, I won't even open your mail. I publish your work; the least you can do is get your facts straight.

How can you turn a regional editor off? By doing silly things. By making small mistakes that you wouldn't have made if you really thought about it. By being lazy or unimaginative or overenthusiastic or careless.

I can think of only one exception to all that. It was an opening paragraph of a query letter from a gentleman who obviously gave his article idea an enormous amount of thought, research, care and enthusiasm. The opening paragraph went like this:

> It was a native Vermonter who, in 1864 during the Civil War, asked the Congress, with a hint of Vermont frugality, "to what end more useful and grand and at the same time simple and inexpensive can we devote the Chamber than to ordain that it shall be set apart for the reception of such statuary as each state shall elect deserving of this lasting commemoration?"

What the native Vermonter wanted in 1864, I finally figured out, was statues from all the states of the current union to adorn the halls of Congress.

But I won't tell you I figured that out in a hurry. Anyone who could open a query letter with a sentence that tortured and yet that fervid deserved better than a quick dismissal.

I wrote the gentleman one of my nicest rejection slips. He hadn't turned me off. He made me smile.

Leads That Absolutely Won't Work

The following leads are suicidal, and especially so in regional publications because regional readers need extra coaxing. They have a tendency to skim. Avoid, at all costs, the following:

1. *The Oldest Chestnut of Them All*
   "According to *Webster's New Collegiate Dictionary*, 'courage' means 'that quality of mind which. . . .'" Etc.

2. *The Uninspired Quote*
   " 'I'm confused. I really can't make up my mind,' said 23-year-old blacksmith, Linda Quarles."

3. *The Belabored Scene-Setter*
   "A slight breeze stirred the dead leaves on the frozen ground as storm clouds threatened overhead. The village green, so recently the scene of joyous activity, was vacant and sere. Scarcely a sound could be heard. The end was in sight."

4. *The Second Oldest Chestnut of Them All*
   "Harry and Mary Perry had a dream—an impossible dream most people thought—but this year that impossible dream became reality."

5. *The Too-Cute-to-Be-True Lead*
   "This is a whale of a tale about the tail of a whale."

6. *The Too-Thin-to-Be-Believed Quote*
   "A shake-up in the government of Connecticut, rumored to affect bureaucrats and appointed officials in all levels, is expected to occur in the foreseeable future, according to usually reliable sources."

7. *The Condescending Come-On*
   "Before you turn the page, read these next few paragraphs. They may very well change your life."

8. *The Lead that Begs to Be Ignored*
   "I'm not much of a writer—never have been. I have never published anything before, and am not likely to again. But I have something I really want to say about cut glass, and I hope you'll take time out from your busy life to read about it."

9. *The Third Oldest Chestnut of Them All*
   "When Montpelier High School and Barre's Spaulding High School get together for a football game, you can throw the record books out the window."

10. *The Lead That Bids To Be Ignored*
    The Salinas Valley is in Northern California. It is a long narrow swale between two ranges of mountains and the Salinas River winds and twists up the center until it falls into the Monterey Bay.*

*This is the lead to *East of Eden* by John Steinbeck, a book that becomes markedly more engaging immediately after these two tedious sentences.

4

How to Turn an Editor On

Mastering regional magazine marketing

There is an ugly rumor that circulates among freelance writers that I would like to address myself to, and eliminate.

Rumor has it that editors of regional magazines like to edit. They enjoy meddling with copy, changing words and reshaping style. Rumor has it that we don't feel fulfilled unless we can editorially dabble at least once on every page we plan to publish.

That's absolute nonsense. Editors of regional magazines aren't anxious to edit at all. It's an aggravating chore that takes time and bogs us down. We like to make assignments. We enjoy planning future issues. We love reading complimentary mail, or unsolicited mentions of our publications in newspapers. But edit copy? It's a nuisance, and we do it only when we have to. That's not just my opinion: it's a generally held one.

So what is one sure way of turning an editor on? Write copy that doesn't need to be edited. You start by making certain you and your editor's story expectations coincide. Then you research that story thoroughly. Finally, you sit down in front of your typewriter—a good dictionary, thesaurus or synonym finder, and your notes close at hand—and you type. It might take one draft or it might take ten. Just make certain that the copy you finally send to the editor is clear, clean, precise, concise, rhythmical, grammatical, and filled with strong words and phrases. Include all of this and you will have won the admiration and respect of someone who is in the position to give you another assignment down the road. And another.

Make the copy clear in direction and intent. Make it obvious from the top what you're talking about. Regional publications don't have the luxury or the inclination to indulge their writers with ponderous, mysterious, rambling, wandering openings. We want our writers to be articulate and cogent from the very start right to the very end.

Somewhere near the start, there should be something I call "the billboard paragraph"—which often makes the difference between an article succeeding nicely or failing miserably.

Billboards do what their name implies. They flash a message, catch people's interest, and promote a product—all in a few seconds. They succinctly summarize the article. They tell the reader, in a single paragraph, what he is about to read. Every magazine article must make its intentions known early because readers want to know what they are going to read about. That is especially true in regional publications where readers often have the tendency to be simply viewers. If we regional editors are going to entice our readers into investing some time in the prose we have prepared for them, we have to let them know quickly what the nature and value of that investment is. That is what happens in a billboard. The writer makes his intentions known. Practically no one reads a magazine cover to cover: we're all selective. Billboards help us to select. The lead paragraphs of an article are like the opening lines of a play. But before that play gets too far along, a narrator steps from behind the curtain and explains to the audience in simple sentences what the play will be about.

A billboard paragraph in a magazine article serves as that narration.

An example of a lead and billboard from a piece I published in *Ms.* magazine:

> Monogamy is something I have never given a lot of thought to until recently when, rather unexpectedly but very explicitly, I got propositioned. It was not at all a professional offer. The woman who was making it was lovely and charming. Neither was it an offer I could brush off effortlessly. In fact, it was an invitation I toyed with for more than a moment.

That was the opening paragraph. It was intended to generate immediate reader interest. "Does he or doesn't he?" I wanted my readers to be asking. Then I presented them with the billboard.

> But eventually I said what I knew I would say from the beginning. I said no. I thanked her for what I considered to be a very high compliment and said for the first time in my life—that my wife and I are into fidelity. We practice it on a regular basis. Perhaps it's for lack of imagination but we take our terribly conventional marriage vows seriously. So thank you—really—I said. But no.

That was the billboard. The article went on at some length on the virtues of a closed marriage versus an open one. I thought it had lots of good stuff in it and I hope *Ms.* readers followed the piece to its last word. But they knew right from the beginning that that was what they were going to get. They knew by the end of my second paragraph—my billboard— that the piece was going to be about fidelity. If marital infidelity held more charm for them, they could quickly turn the pages of that edition of *Ms.* (which was devoted entirely to issues of sex) and read on. They had invested only two paragraphs of time in what I had to offer.

Here's the lead we ran by author Teri Swenson Curtis:

> "All you have to do is run like crazy straight down the hill.
> Ready? Okay. Let's go." Somehow those words found their
> way into my mind, which I thought I was losing, and made
> my body react accordingly. I was aware only of a pounding in
> my throat and two wild eyes (mine) staring at the gravel
> parking lot in which I was to land, 1,200 feet later. The next
> thing I knew, I was flying.

That's my idea of a strong lead. The next paragraph contained the billboard.

> Hang gliding is a rapidly growing sport all over the country
> and Vermont is certainly no exception.

That is an excellent billboard. You know that a female writer with a light touch and a flair for the dramatic is going to tell you about hang gliding in Vermont. She's given you the capsule summary.

Some subject matter is neither difficult nor emotional, but writers still need to set a mood, set their readers up, and insure their interest. Here's how Jim McElholm began an article called "North by East."

> If the local assessors have done their job promptly, readers
> of *Down East* who own property in Maine will be receiving
> their tax bills about the same time this issue of the magazine
> arrives in the mail. We only hope that the pleasure to be found
> in our pages will help offset the pain in the other missive.

That has a nice twist to it. It makes the reader sit and think, which is exactly what the writer wants him to do. "Let's see. If the local assessors have done their jobs promptly, then I'll get my tax bill when I get my copy of *Down East*. Okay. And *Down East* came this morning. And I do find pleasure in its pages. So that means. . .Oh rats!"

Score one for a clever writer.

How about this lead we carried in a recent article on bee lining, "The Art of Tracking Wild Bees and Their Honey"?

> "It has to be in your blood," explains Bill Matson. The

statement is the best reason I have come across why anyone would knowingly enter an apiary—anytime. Any time except the first, which can be written off to curiosity. And I've been reaching for a reason ever since I began keeping bees six years ago.

The author, Lance Khouri, let you know right away that his article would be slightly whimsical, quite personal, and a pleasure to read. He also did himself the favor of jumping in with both feet.

His name is Dave and he's 165 pounds of rompin' stompin' dynamite on a Denver Saturday night. During the week, he sells shoes; but at night and on weekends, Dave turns cowboy.

That was the lead paragraph of "Riding the Neon Electric Range" by Will Keener, published in *Denver Monthly*. The author went right to Dave's heart and soul with his opening, and right to our high interest. We want to know more about this shoe salesman of the range. We're immediately drawn into the story, by some very simple, straightforward sentences.

Kathi Fisher, writing in *Austin*, a Texas city magazine, began her story on the handicapped and their participation in Austin's leisure activities this way:

Can a blind man play baseball?
Does a bear live in the woods?

What a lovely breakthrough. The author has taken a serious question—adaptive programs for the handicapped and how can they be best put into action—and made a little piece of humor happen. She defused an emotional situation right off the bat, and *then* plunged into a discussion of the fact that yes, in Austin under a new program for the handicapped, a blind man *can* play baseball. They do, all summer long.

In keeping with that magazine's upbeat image, freelance writer Kay Maughan opened her piece in *Nashville!* on couples who have been happily married this way:

> With statistics telling us that marriage is a losing proposition one third of the time and with books telling us that marriage has to change to be viable in today's society, we decided to sit down and talk with four Nashville couples who've been making it work through all the cultural changes. These four couples have been all together more than 30 years. They're in love. And they're all different.

That's a lead and a billboard wrapped into one paragraph. It has a little sentimentalism. It's positive. It forecasts good news. It predicts pleasant memories are coming. It repeats certain words for emphasis and it uses a perfectly delightful non-sentence. All in all, that's a mighty good lead.

You can turn your editor on by making your copy clear right from the beginning. And right to the very end.

Make your copy clean. That doesn't mean you have to keep retyping and retyping until you produce immaculate pages. A little pencil editing on typewritten copy won't hurt you. In fact, I like to see authors who have done a little pencil editing on articles I've assigned to them. It shows me that they read the draft they have written and made a few improvements. But let me stress the word "little" and the word "few" that precede "pencil editing" and "improvements." A lot of pencil editing is messy and editors have enough problems without dealing with messes. Turn us on by making your copy clean.

Make your copy precise. Get your facts right. Regionals almost never have research staffs. Our editorial departments and budgets are too limited to allow us the luxury of copy checkers and research assistants. We're very dependent on the reliability and accuracy of our contributors. Make us happy and stay reliable. Double-check your facts. If there's a quote you think might be questionable, either don't use it or call the subject up on the telephone and elicit the quote again. If there's a spelling you're not sure of, don't assume the editor will correct it for you. Do *all* the necessasy homework.

One way to double-check factual accuracy is to allow the subject of an article to read the piece before it's sent off to the regional publication. I advise against that practice in practically every instance, but some editors don't mind it at all. (My objection is that if a writer knows his subject is going to pre-read and, in effect, have censorship power, the writer will aim his words at the subject and not at the magazine's audience. There are exceptions of course. If Alexander Solzhenitsyn, who lifes in Cavendish, Vermont, allowed a *Vermont Life* writer to interview him, I'd give him all the censorship power he could possibly want. And if he left Russia for the reasons he *said* he left, he wouldn't want any.)

Make your copy concise. Don't say it in one thousand words if it can be said just as nicely in five hundred. Avoid unnecessary adverbs and adjectives. Avoid pairs of words that mean the same thing, like "null and void" or "each and every." Assume the worst about the readers of the article you are writing. Assume that if a paragraph you have just created could *possibly* be misunderstood, it will be. Write it over again so that you are certain the possibility has been eliminated. If something sounds awkward, unclear, or long-winded, you need to rewrite it. One of the best ways to find out if your copy is any of the above is to read it aloud. If it *sounds* superfluous and redundant, then it is.

Remember that regional publications want to get their messages across directly and with energy and animation. Concise prose fills that bill. (The exception is the major city magazine which occasionally carries lengthy pieces— generally of an exploitive or expose nature.)

Make your copy rhythmical. Vary the sentence structure and length. Keep paragraphs on the short side. (Long paragraphs are hard on the eye and tend to make readers lose attention. Regional editors want more than anything else to keep their readers' attention.) Make the prose flow with tempo and style. If you have to choose between being a little poetic or a little turgid, go with the former. Your editor will be ever so grateful.

Make your copy grammatical. Speaking before the Bread Loaf School in Middlebury, Vermont, during the summer of 1961, the eminent poet Robert Frost said: "You don't have to know how to spell to write poetry. You can be rather loose in your syntax as far as I'm concerned. You don't have to know how to punctuate at all." But Frost was talking about poetry. And there are some poetry editors around who would take strong exception to his disdainful approach to the rules and regulations of his mother tongue.

I'm a prose editor and I take strong exception. When I see an article overrun with bad grammar, I assume that the author is either lazy or ignorant. To the best of my knowledge, I have never purchased a single article from anyone who had either of those character deficiencies.

Punch-up your prose with strong words and phrases. While writing the chapter you are now reading, I have referred eight times to a book titled *The Synonym Finder* published by Rodale Press. In each case, I needed a word that was better and stronger than the one that immediately came into my head and so I went for help. And I found it. A few paragraphs ago, you read this sentence: "If you have to choose between being a little poetic or a little turgid, go with the former." I got "turgid" out of my good friend and finder of synonyms because "wordy" is a weak word. "Turgid" is much stronger. Try substituting "saunter," "strut," "limp," or "march" for "walk." And "absence" or "lack of" sounds much better than "don't have." Small changes like this can improve your image as a writer.

Fight for the best possible word. Read phrases over and over. Don't settle for a good word when a better one is out there begging to be used. Keep *Bartlett's Familiar Quotations* near your writing hands. (Not as near as your thesaurus and dictionary, but close.) Consult it when you need help from someone who has already penned a quotation worthy of being familiar. If you're writing about age, for example, check "age" in Bartlett's index. Shakespeare said some lovely things about growing old, and so did the Old

Testament, Yeats, Freud, and Oliver Wendell Holmes. They're all now in public domain—which made John Bartlett a wealthy man. Spread the wealth.

Stay in the active tense as often as possible. "She labored up the craggy mountain" is so much better than "The craggy mountain was labored up by her" or "I will always remember my first visit to Boston" is a great improvement over "My first visit to Boston will always be remembered by me."

Choose action verbs. Say "apply" rather than "make application," "Consider" rather than "give consideration to," "need" rather than "have need of."

Put statements in positive form; make clear-cut assertions. Don't say "He did not agree." Say "He disagreed." Don't say "He didn't remember." Say "He forgot." Don't be evasive by writing "She was not very often on time"; instead write "She usually came late."

Regional publications depend on strong words more than any other group in the medium. We don't have hard news to sell, or fiction, or sensationalism. We need sentences and articles that have had all the clichés and jargon trimmed away, leaving only bright, sharp, descriptive prose. We are looking for articles that are clear, clean, precise, concise, rhythmical, grammatical, and filled with strong words and phrases. That turns us on.

Oh Query Me, Query Me

But before you get that far in the process, you should have an assignment—or at least an offer from an editor to look at your writing on speculation. You have to turn an editor on with your query. Here's one that turned me on:

> When Gertrude Lepine was young she taught school in Stowe Hollow. But early one spring day—one of those clear, sunny days that can only happen in Vermont, when the air is flavorful and the maple sap is running—Gertrude walked out, leaving classroom walls for the family farm.
> She has never looked back.
> Today Gertrude milks 70 Jersey cows. Her hard work and

enthusiasm have made her a successful dairy farmer, no mean accomplishment for any *man* in the back hills of Morristown. Gertrude is a lady.

Helping her in the barn every day are her two sisters—Jeannette and Therese. Jeannette was a stewardess for 11 years .with Pan American. Therese started her career as a WAVE and was stationed in Hawaii. *La grande dame de famille*, Imelda Lepine, comes down to the barn, too. Visitors quickly find that her specialty is fresh, homemade doughnuts bequeathed to grateful grandchildren. And to occasional visitors, if there are enough to go around. The grandchildren come first.

Would you be interested in a story on the Lepine women of Mount Sterling View Farm? They are women who combine worldliness and intelligence with the persistence and stamina of their French-Canadian ancestors.

I have studied at Bennington College and the University of Vermont and am presently a correspondent for the *Burlington Free Press*.

Thank you for your consideration.

I called the writer of that query the morning I received it and made the assignment on the spot. *Everything* about that query turned me on.

For one thing, it was intelligently written. The lead paragraph was nicely lyrical. (Remember, lead paragraphs in queries are as important as they are in subsequent articles—or as important as they are in letters to wealthy relatives who dimly remember you, for that matter.)

The query also had a billboard. The third paragraph gave me a nice summary of what the entire query was so successfully presenting.

I liked the idea of four women working a dairy farm because I never saw a story like that in *Vermont Life* before. I liked the fact that it was a family operation and that there was a nice mix of generations to be included in the story. I liked the little phrase in French—*la grande dame de famille*—just because that was *agréable*. I liked the fact that the women were French-Canadians, not only because that is the source of my ancestry also, but because French-Canadians are a minority group in Vermont who don't get much publicity. I liked the fact that the author said she *attended* college and a university. Neither the author nor I have college degrees and I liked her honesty about that fact. I liked the fact that she was a correspondent for one of Vermont's major newspapers. That's a great credential as far as I'm concerned.

There was nothing about that query that I didn't feel good about. I *had* to make that assignment.

Here's another query that turned me on in a hurry:

> Did you know that Vermont has seven living ex-governors? Don't you think it would make sense to get them in a room and talk about how Vermont, with its reputation for frugality and conservatism, is one of the most progressive states in the union? Let's get them together and see what happens.

Did I think that made sense? I certainly did.
Here's a query that carried clout:

> Would you be interested in an article about a monument to love tucked away in Proctor, Vt.?
>
> Wilson Castle was built for a bride. Doctor John Johnson met and fell in love with a woman of noble birth during a visit to England. She agreed to marry him but was heartbroken about traveling to America and never seeing her beloved homeland again. The Doctor's deep love—and not unsubstantial net worth—prompted him to build a castle in his home town of Proctor in 1867. The castle was eventually acquired by the Wilson family who renamed the estate and have called it home for five generations.
>
> The castle has three floors, divided into 32 richly decorated rooms. The antiques and museum pieces reflect the flavor of both the Far East and Europe. The 115-acre estate also includes barns, stables, a carriage house, gas house, and an aviary inhabited by prized Indian peacocks.
>
> The article could open by touching on the romantic history of the castle. The body of the text could deal with descriptions of several of the more striking rooms. An overview of the castle's exterior could also be included. The piece can be concluded with an echo ending.

If you are interested in such an article, I would be glad to submit a 1,500 word piece—on speculation, of course.

Was I interested? Why not? The writer wrote intelligently, the subject matter seemed fascinating, and the piece would arrive in my office with no strings attached. It was being written on speculation. Of *course* I wanted to see it. (There are varying opinions about writing on speculation. I do—all the time—and my credits include most of the major magazines in America. If I have an idea for an article that I think is worth writing, and if I get an expression of interest from an editor, I will certainly sit down and develop the piece. If it gets turned down by the original source, I'll look for a similar publication and try to sell it to them. I've rarely written a piece that I didn't sell *somewhere*. Then again, some of the magazines in which some of my articles have finally appeared are not yet household words.)

Editors are turned on by writers who know their publications. The Wilson Castle query suggested that the article would be 1,500 words, which is *precisely* the length I usually look for. The writer know that I have a mild interest in nicely flavored history but that mostly I was going to be intrigued by the here and now. So did the writer of the ex-governors' query. I share that preference with all regional editors. We're generally promoting and presenting current realities but keeping hints and traces of nostalgia. "We're not interested in 'The Good Old Days' for their own sake," says the editor of *Tar Heel: The Magazine of North Carolina*. "But rather for what they add to the experience of being in North Carolina now."

Both the writers offered their pieces on speculation, which made them most attractive to me. If they had asked for the assignment instead, I probably would have asked for writing credentials and asked to see some examples of previously published work. I'm reluctant to promise the magazine's money to people I don't know and I *hate* paying kill fees.

"The best query I get is from a person with either a track record for good writing and reporting or the promise and dedication of an enthusiastic beginner," says Richard Lwenstein (sic) of the *St. Louis Journalism Review*. I couldn't agree more. A beginner's enthusiasm often compensates for lack of polish.

> Hi, my name is Amy and I'm 11 years old and live in Craftsbury, Vt. I wouldn't want to live any other place in the world.

Eleven-year-old Amy wasn't offering a complicated lead, but I was charmed by her directness.

In this chapter's final words, I want to write about final words. They take almost as much discipline and call for as much impact and energy as do opening words and lead paragraphs.

For some reason that has, thus far in my editorial career, thoroughly escaped me, regional magazine articles seem more often than not to end with a whimper, a fizzle, or a dull thud. So many articles in regional magazines seem to pack all the really good stuff up front and let the tail of the tale quietly fall limp.

I suppose part of the reason for that is human frailty. The writer has run out of things to say and brings his piece to a close in that vacuum. The editor, who might have had to work pretty hard to whip the piece into shape in the first place, probably ran out of stamina by the time he got to the last page of the manuscript. And so the piece just sort of dies out.

Perhaps this is a personal bias that has no universal application, but I *insist* on energized endings. In his article, "Life in a Foxhole" for *Alaska* magazine, Stephen J. Krasemann—one of that state's best-known wildlife photographers—ended a photo essay like this:

> On the day I was scheduled to leave, almost as if to say "You're one of the family," the male came up to me with a vole [a mouselike rodent] in his mouth. He dropped it at my feet. When I didn't pick it up immediately, he pushed it closer—onto the top of my foot.

I thanked him, his family and fate for the chance to travel with and photograph these foxes.

Boston, a monthly that delights in "exclusive reports" and long investigative narratives, ran a 4,000 word beauty called "The Mystery of the UMass Tower." Reporter Ron Winslow went into great detail on why women working in a chemical research laboratory were being struck with a bizarre sickness. He interviewed (doctors, lawyers, and patients), gave case histories, and established that indeed, something inexplicable was happening. He ended with a quote.

> "It's still not clear," he said, "that we have a work related problem. It's still not clear that we have a health problem."

Winslow ended with a question mark. The reader is left ultimately in the dark, right where the writer wanted him to be. Why? Because the sickness in the UMass Tower *is* mysterious. There was no precise explanation for it. Winslow tailored his ending to his piece.

On the other hand, Minda O'Mary wanted to be precise in her article "The Portable Feast" (*San Diego* magazine) describing "epicurean inspirations for a stadium afternoon." After suggesting portable picnic possibilities that even made me drool—and I can't stand picnics—she simply said "ta,ta."

> When the game is over, simply pack up and head for home. No need to worry about fighting traffic to a nearby restaurant. You'll certainly have won points with your guests who will remember the feast, long after they've forgotten the score.

D magazine (published in the Dallas, Fort Worth area) ran an article called "Owning a Piece of the Rockies" with the subhead, "How Harry Bass Got to Be King of the Mountain." The article, skillfully written by Lindsay Heinsen, told how a Texas playground, called Colorado, was invaded by all sorts of land investors. Texas oilman Harry Bass was just one of them, and not at all a bad fellow.

She ended her piece like this:

> "If I wanted to make a lot of money, I'd probably entertain

the idea of selling our holdings in Vail Associates, but once you sell it, what do you do with the profit?

"There are risks involved in any investment. I'd just as soon get into something that's not going to wear out, that we know fairly well and stick with." And be king of the mountain.

The author did Harry no wrong. She quoted him accurately, ended with a magnificent non-sentence that tied her piece back into the subhead, and exited gracefully.

Pay careful attention to the end. Make your last words count. And make them as appropriate and as impact-full as the last words in these articles.

* * *

If you want to turn on an editor with your ideas, just remember that editors make their living with words. Make certain *your* words to the editor are full of life.

5

Write Up Their Alley

Secrets of a salable regional article

Every article you will read in any publication, ever, began as an idea. The idea may have formed first in the mind of an editor who passed it along to a writer he thought capable of developing it into something readable. It may have first appeared in the mind of a writer who convinced an editor that it was worthy of extension and exploitation, or it may have been passed along. Sons-in-law sometimes have ideas that get lateraled to their wives' literary-minded mothers, and shop foremen sometimes have ideas they share with writer/assembly-line workers over a few beers after work. The development may be by a team of writers or by a bevy of editors. But in the beginning, every finished article that will ever be, and that ever was, was an idea. Somebody had to come up with it.

Should that somebody be you?

More to the point, how often have you read something somewhere and thought, "Damn. Why didn't I think of that? I could have written it with much more spirit." Doesn't that happen all the time? It does to me and I'm one of the most active (part-time) freelance writers I know. I'm always seeing articles written by someone else that should have been written by me.

I remember one evening at home when everyone else was asleep and I was waiting to get tired, I pulled out a small electronic thirty-dollar football game—it's something to amuse myself while waiting for my mind to wind down. But on this particular occasion I didn't play with the game very long: I had mastered it weeks ago—could score a touchdown any time I wanted to by directing my little blipping halfback around all the little blipping defensive players. It wasn't really fun anymore. Even when I played against neighborhood kids who got really excited controlling little flashes of light in a plastic box, it wasn't fun. I had to cheat to lose, that's how good I was. I had to run into their blipping defense on purpose, just to keep things interesting. It was like Notre Dame playing Vassar. I was, easily, the best computerized football player in the country.

And then it hit me. There's a story. There's a piece in that—"The World's Champion Computerized Football Player, and Who Cares?" I could see it so clearly—a little caustic humor, some self-muckracking; I'd admit sheepishly that I attained my lofty status with computerized football because I'd spent a lot of time not sleeping. Then I'd talk about the strategy in computerized football and wagering and hustling. A magnificent story. I couldn't wait to write it.

But I did want an expression of interest. When I have a story idea like that, I want some editor somewhere to say, "We'll look at it." I don't need more of an obligation than that, but I do need a hint of encouragement. So the next morning I called an acquaintance who is an editor of *Playboy*. I had thought Mr. Hefner's magazine would probably be the place to start with that idea: with the men's angle and humor, it would be right for them. I knew this particular editor would prefer to have me write him, but the idea was good. I wanted some immediate feedback.

I got it. *Playboy* had assigned "The World's Champion Computerized Football Player" story months earlier. "To whom?" I asked in a voice that did not hide my dismay. The editor told me.

"You're kidding!" I said. "I write circles around that guy." That was a stupid thing to say and I immediately regretted it. Writers who compare themselves favorably to other writers get on editors' nerves.

I tried to make amends. "I mean he's good. There's no question about that. But, man, this story was *made* for me."

"Well, it may have been made for you, but it was assigned to him. Keep in touch." End of conversation.

I was going to have to reslant the story and sell it somewhere else. How could it be restructured? Maybe make it a touch more cerebral. Something about how American males are getting addicted to computerized games. But that's not really unlike our addiction to any other noncomputerized game in years gone by. Nice angle. *Esquire* maybe or *Saturday Review*, possibly even *Harper's*.

Rejection slips, rejection slips, rejection slips. (I had sent multiple queries—which is normally against my ethics—but I didn't want to lose another assignment to time.) Nice idea, editors said, but not a new idea.

I never wrote that story. My original, clear inspiration was twisted and crushed to fit one publication or another, and it wasn't clever anymore. The life had gone out of it. No one was interested.

Editors are not interested in old ideas. Or ideas whose time has come, and gone. That couldn't be more important than it is in regional magazines where topicality and timeliness are crucial. It becomes increasingly significant to magazines that appear infrequently. *Vermont Life*, a quarterly, has to plan stories a year in advance of publication. Since we tie our publication to the seasons, articles which are written one winter see print in the winter following. With that kind of time lag built into the publishing cycle, it is obvious why a slightly warm idea holds absolutely no charm for me.

Nor does it for any other editor. Even regionals that reflect on the past want their current stories relevant. "We're not interested in the good old days for their own sake," says James Wise, editor of *Tar Heel: The Magazine of North Carolina*. "We're interested in what they add to the experience of being a North Carolinian now."

Editors are looking for something new. "What new or fresh slant does a proposed article bring to an industry or company?" asks Ed Sullivan, editor of *Seattle Business Magazine*. "That's what I'm looking for."

"Little-known facts of Nevada history," said the editor of *The Nevadan*, a supplement of the *Las Vegas Review-Journal Nevadan*. "We like to probe the unknown."

As an editor, I have occasionally been guilty of using the line, "great idea, but we've already got it in the works," as an excuse to a writer whose feelings I didn't want to hurt. When a good, proven writer comes in with an idea that is already assigned to an unknown writer, I feel a little bit saddened.

"Where were you last month when this was going on?"

"Busy with that story you assigned me," the proven-good writer says.

"Oh, yeah, that."

Get percolating early. Get ideas to editors before anyone else does. Get the promise of an assignment—or at least a read-through—before the other fellow beats you out of it. I have some rules for spotting good ideas that should help:

1. Be a people watcher. Keep an eye out for mannerisms, similarities, differences—fodder for a comparative article. What are people dressing like? What styles are returning? How is the language in your region changing and why? An article appearing in *Pittsburgh* is entitled "Do You Belong in Pittsburg? We're Asking You and Other Experts." Has that question been asked in your region?

2. Pay close attention to what people read (or intend to read). You can capitalize on other peoples' ideas, and when those other people are writers, that's perfectly fair. "What is Being Read in New Orleans?" would certainly interest the editor of *New Orleans*.

3. Read your newspaper for the story behind the story. Don't assume that the professional reporter got the whole thing. He didn't. He didn't have the time. You do.

4. Pay attention to the seasons. If your region has seasons, play off them. How are ski slopes utilized in August? Where do professional athletes go when the season's over? Where do sailboats go in February? What do farmers do when it's too cold to work outside?

5. Be on the lookout for the unobvious profile. A conversation with a noncelebrity is almost invariably more interesting than one with someone familiar with interviewers and interviewing techniques. But bankers, stockbrokers, architects, doctors, lawyers, ministers, housewives, and all the other people who aren't usually the subject of interviews would probably consent to one if you said your regional magazine had agreed to consider a piece on that person. (Don't say the magazine sent you unless it actually did. When I find out that someone said he was reporting for *Cincinnati* when actually he was writing on speculation, I write his name on a piece of paper, and the paper is edged in black.) There is one sure trick for getting people to talk about themselves: ask them to.

6. Combine nostalgia with futurism. This seems to be capable of creating some sparks. Interview a former governor and a would-be governor. Put a retired newspaper editor in a room with a cub reporter and watch things happen. Has your regional ever done a piece on the local chiropractors versus the teaching doctors at the nearest medical school?

7. Read the yellow pages of the telephone directory. If you're absolutely stuck for a good story idea, and something in them doesn't fire up your imagination, you should probably check with a doctor or a chiropractor.

8. Read Writer's Digest. Obvious, but the magazine publishes idea lists that are extremely valuable. It also reports on which editors are buying what articles and is full of handy hints to better writing.

9. Be aware of how your own life is one story after another. Some days your life is eight stories. When they are self-pitying stories no one over in the regional publication's editorial office is likely to be terribly interested. But if you can combine humor and regionalism you're going to find an editor eager to give you work. Regional editors bemoan the lack of light, topical writing applicable to their area. It's so rare and we wish it weren't.

10. Don't surround yourself with writers. I used to, and it was terribly frustrating. Not that writers aren't nice people: a fair percentage of them are, but they—I mean we—tend to get a little singleminded when we are with people who share our avocation. And a little competitive.

"What do'ya have going these days, Pete?"

"Oh, I don't know. The Solzhenitsyn interview looks like a possibility. How about you?"

"Well, I'm pretty much up to my ears. *National Geographic* is trying to get me to go to Switzerland. But you know, living out of a suitcase, every meal in a restaurant, it gets to be too much."

Writers don't stimulate other writers to produce greater and greater work. Writers stimulate other writers to produce greater and more outrageous flapdoodle. Hang around with insurance salesmen and school teachers, pool hustlers and zoo keepers, engineers and entrepreneurs. You won't be so compelled to compete with them. And they are much more likely to help you develop salable story ideas.

11. Block out time when you will absolutely not permit yourself to think about writing. . . .That could be a weekend, or a week, or the month of April, but make certain that you take a vacation from the strain of trying to think of something new all the time. Give your brain a chance to relax. Refreshed, it will serve you infinitely better.

The Importance of Being Timely

When authors ask me what my lead time is, I generally say "six months," which is half false in two different ways and two different directions. Our winter issue comes out in late November, which means we have to be just about ready to be on the press by mid-October. That gives us time to get shipping labels and instructions to our printer and gives us some lead time to get subscription copies mailed. (We like subscribers and newsstand buyers to receive their copies of the magazine in the same week. That cuts down on hard feelings.)

Given time for editing, sending first drafts back to authors for touch-ups, copyediting, sending articles for typesetting, giving galleys to the art director for layouts, and reading page proofs, we really ought to have all copy for a winter issue of *Vermont Life* in the house by early June. That would indicate that, indeed, we have a six-month lead time.

But if I ever had all my winter copy available for typesetting by early June, the aforementioned Linda Paradee—the managing editor—would drop over in a dead faint. She's not used to that kind of propitiousness from me.

There have been times, in fact, in which I have handed over copy for typesetting as late as mid-September for a winter issue. That doesn't make the typesetter very happy nor does it amuse Paradee. That also doesn't mean we really have a *two*-month lead time. But in emergency situations— when there is something late-breaking that means an article has to be changed or ditched entirely—it can be done. We can get away with a change two months before our publication date.

But what is the *true* lead time for a winter story? It should be the previous winter. Since *Vermont Life* is a seasonal magazine and depends very much on seasonal nuances in order to make its regional point, winter articles should be written in the winter. Certainly they have to be *photographed* in the winter. That might not be true for *San Diego* magazine—a monthly publication that tells of a city whose summers are very warm and rather dry and whose winters are very dry and rather warm. A little seasonal cheating is allowed in Southern California.

But in Vermont, the season can't be faked. I won't allow an orange- and yellow-leafed tree to appear in the corner of a photograph that purports to show the town of Springfield in springtime. Similarly, I discourage writers from attempting to conjure up a tale of gathering maple sap for a sugar-on-snow party while reclining poolside in the middle of July. The editor of *Cincinnati* magazine is not interested in a piece about the importance of Tom Seaver's fast ball near the end of a pennant race if it was written last February.

Get to know the real lead time of the regional you are interested in contributing to, and then consider the variables.

Is the magazine geared to the season, the months, topical events, or timeless themes? Does the editor want to look at material a year before it can be published—as I often do—or five days before it is published, as editors of many newspaper supplements are able to do? Is there a firm lead time? Find out what it is. A November story that misses the November deadline either gets killed altogether or sits in the files for a year. Because most regional magazines pay upon publication, not acceptance (more than two-thirds, according to the survey, time is of the essence. Don't lose out on a good story, an important by-line, and a handsome paycheck just because you failed to keep an eye on the calendar or contact your key interview subject before he left on a six-month cruise up the Amazon.

And don't lose a good story because you assume someone has already written it. That's one of the reasons query letters were invented. It never hurts to ask.

The Importance of Research

Researching is a matter of style. My style has always been to stay away from topics about which I am totally ignorant. I write best about things that I know without studying—like my own special corner of the landscape, my family, or my job.

When Judson Hale, editor of *Yankee*, asked me to write a piece on the Lake Champlain monster (a cousin of the Loch Ness beastie and just as likely), I went to our local high school and asked an English teacher to nominate a good researcher for me. He introduced me to a young woman, and I said to her: "I've been offered $600 to write about the Lake Champlain monster. Find our everything you can about it, and I'll split the fee with you."

She found out a lot, and gave me a dozen pages of notes. From them, I was able to write my piece in a single Saturday afternoon. I think three hundred bucks isn't bad for that period of time. And my researcher was delighted with her profit. (Later, when *Reader's Digest* picked up the Lake Champlain monster story and gave me an additional $1,000, I had some question about splitting *that*, too. And I'm not about to admit what my final decision was. But *boy*, that was a good Saturday afternoon.)

If you'd rather do your own research, and most writers are inclined that way, don't waste time in the library when a simple phone call will do. Don't get involved in nuts and bolts if nuts and bolts aren't called for in the article you are putting together. Catharine Findiesen wrote a piece for *Vermont Life* on what Vermont looks like from the air. "Looking Down on Vermont, Lovingly" *could* have been an article on the geological formations that have caused the state's topography to swell and decline. It *could* have been an article on migration patterns and how various immigrants to Vermont laid their architectural fingerprints on the countryside. It *could* have been piece about rural and urban sprawl and how planning directors are attempting to regulate the growth of suburbia and limit the destruction of farm property.

Instead, this remarkable writer asked her father—who happens to own a 1947 Champ airplane—to take her for a ride. When the ride was over, she wrote about what Vermont looked like from above. She wrote about it lovingly, and it was just what I wanted it to be. She also saved herself countless, wasted hours in a library.

If your father doesn't own an airplane, find someone who does. When researching an article, ask yourself this question: "If I had to answer these questions by tomorrow at noon, how would I proceed?" Then simply proceed that way. Regional editors don't want their readers to trip over a lot of useless, laboriously gathered information. We don't want our writers to tarry over tedious details. If you're writing a piece on the Pope's last visit to New York, don't call the chamber of commerce or the *New York Times*. Call the Vatican. If you're writing a piece on Indiana's first experiments in hydroelectric power, call someone who was involved in those experiments. If you're writing about South Carolina's earliest settlers, call South Carolina's state archeologist. Go for it. Go right for the top. The *worst* thing that can happen is that the person you are calling will not accept your call.

"She's not in right now, may I tell her who's calling?" an officious secretary may say (in the worst of all situations).

"Sure. Tell her I'm trying to research South Carolina's earliest settlers for *Sandpiper* magazine and I really need some help," you could respond.

"Oh," the secretary will respond, somewhat more alertly. "I think she's in now. One moment and I'll connect you."

Research can be farmed out. It also can be overdone. Think of yourself as a hired hand when you do your own research. And think also about the publication you're writing for and what your pay is likely to be. If you have been offered $100 to write about a lemon grove in the Tampa area, five hours research and five hours writing time seems plenty. You shouldn't pay yourself less than $10 an hour unless the by-line you're seeking is going to give you high prestige or unless it's your first.

Hit the Spot: Matching Ideas and Markets

If the editor of *Alaska* reads a manuscript about strict Eskimo parents who tell their children to come home before dark, he will know the writer is a stranger to the land of the midnight sun. The editor of *Texas Highways* has no use for stories or photographs that explore the road-damaging effects of snow and frost. You've simply got to know the territory.

Let's say oil was discovered outside Decatur, Georgia. You heard it on the radio driving to work this morning. You work in Atlanta, not too far from Decatur, and you do some freelance writing in your spare time. Is there a regional story in the discovery?

Is there! It's a story of national importance: no one knew Georgia was sitting on any oil before. *Time* and *Newsweek* are going to cover this, but don't bother to contact them. They both have Atlanta bureaus and are undoubtedly covering the story with staff writers.

But *Southern Living* would probably not be covering with staff and they would certainly be interested in coverage if the slant was positive and the writing was crisp. How about an in-depth feature on why anyone even thought to *look* for oil outside Decatur. Will the oil be sold locally?

The *Atlantic Journal Constitution* Sunday magazine would be most interested in a piece that told how the discovery would affect local electricity rates. Who will man the oil rigs? *Georgia Life*, people-oriented and genteel, might be interested in a Georgian who wakes up at 5 a.m. and drives out to the new rig. What's he have to say about this unlikely happening? Will it affect Decatur's basic way of life? Over at *Brown's Guide to Georgia*, the new energy supply would be viewed as a visitor's attraction. Are tours of the oil fields available? *Atlanta* magazine would want to know why it took so long to discover that black gold, and the weekly *Atlanta Gazette* would want to know if anyone was making a "windfall" profit from the discovery.

Again, you have to know the territory. And you have to know regional's personalities. That oil story could go to six different places this afternoon. Unless you wait until someone else gets the assignments.

Spotting the story and then selecting the market takes

skill, but the skill comes with reading and practice.

What if the trailer story on the 6 o'clock news showed sheriff's deputies breaking up a moonshine still back in the hills outside Austin, Texas. "Funny little story," the announcer announces, "We don't usually think of fast-paced, modern Austin cradling a moonshiner. But by golly, the deputies saw a funny line of smoke back in the woods, checked it out and found a 50-barrel copper still bubbling away. The main ingredients were corn and sugar and the proprietor had stepped away. And now for the weather. . . ."

Whoa! Wouldn't *Austin* magazine, even though it's run by the Chamber of Commerce, be fascinated with a piece on bootlegging? "We look for articles about interesting businesses and the people who make them interesting," says editor Hal Suskind. "We also look for articles on Austin's entertainment scene."

Well what could be more interesting than a moonshiner's business? Will he set up business again? Will he be found? He certainly used to be part of the entertainment scene.

The same story might make a salable short subject for *Texas Monthly*. They pay $50 to $75 for items in their regular section, "Texas Monthly Reporter," which are mostly supplied by freelancers.

True West magazine, also published in Austin, would like to know about moonshining in and around Austin between 1830 and 1910, but the newly discovered still could be the peg to hang the history on. *The Journal of Southern History*, published by Rice University, would want you to compare the Austin still with their counterparts in Kentucky and West Virginia. *Texas Highways*, published by the state Travel Division, would want to know if the smashed still is currently open to the public, and how one might most scenically arrive there. *Big D* in Dallas and *Houston* magazine would want to know if there are any bootleggers in their area.

Sometimes story ideas shout at you and sometimes they

whisper and sometimes they come with a smile. But when you learn to recognize and market them, freelancing will turn from pre-occupation to occupation. It's a nice transition.

Providing the Decoration

Photos and art

I am not a photographer. I'm also not a painter, illustrator, sculptor, or originator of etchings. These are not talents I possess. But I know a lot about photography, and a little about those other arts, because I deal with many of them every day. Being a firm believer in the philosophy which holds that a person need not know how to *take* good photographs in order to *judge* good photographs, I go about my job with a clear conscience. One major part of my job is to judge photographs—to look for interesting ones where the lighting is good and composition is better, and the subject matter is Vermont and in good taste. My counterparts in regional publications make the same judgments for their magazines. I judge about twenty thousand photographs a year and select about three hundred for publication. I would guess that the editor of *Arizona Highways* judges ten times that number and we are both grateful for the fact that we have talented art directors, but ultimately the decision about whether a photograph gets published or not is the editor's.

Bearing this in mind, if you are a writer who also has photographic inclinations the first question you should ask yourself is: are you really interested in providing the decoration? Is your writing talent complemented by photographic or illustrative talent? By handling both ends of the assignment—the words and the pictures—are you enhancing or endangering the final product? Are you going to be able to do justice to the subject you are covering both photographically and editorially? Or would you be better off sharing the load?

I don't ask those questions to intimidate you. I don't mean to dissuade you from expanding your contribution to the regional magazines you are working for. The money gets twice as good or more when you provide photographs with the words. And there are a number of people who possess both skills. My father was a photographer with an international reputation and I have always been convinced that he wrote better than he shot.

My intention is just to throw some caution at you. My father and others may have been able to write about a subject and photograph that subject at the same time but I know *I* couldn't. When I'm busy taking notes, I don't want a camera hanging around my neck. When I'm hungrily waiting for an interviewee to produce an endearingly quotable quote, I don't want to worry if the sun happens to go behind the clouds. If I'm describing a thunderstorm in a hayfield, it's difficult enough to keep my notes dry. I don't want to be bothered with a damp Nikon or a saturated Canon. Writing is all the work I can handle.

When I have an assignment that requires photographs, I generally ask the editor if I can provide a partner. Some editors prefer assigning a photographer themselves and others say "Sure, you know the area and you know photographers. Hire somebody." Of course the magazine is actually doing the hiring. I'm just doing the picking.

I always go through that procedure with a touch of envy. Photographers are generally paid more than writers—on a day rate rather than a word rate. But, envy aside, I realize they have a skill that I don't and I pick someone who will be right for the assignment. It will be someone whose work I know—whose photographic ability is in evidence either in slides I've seen in my office or published in other magazines. Some photographers work better with people than others. Some can capture magnificent scenics but get gun-shy around human subjects. Others are able to make people relax, and forget they are being photographed. Still other photographers know how to seemingly disappear, and while I've seen it happen many times, it's a trick I could never explain. I never saw my good friend Richard Howard on the day I got married. Never laid eyes on him. But a week after the wedding, he presented Nancy and me with beautiful black and white prints of the ceremony and the subsequent subdued bacchanal. And sure enough, I was in about half the pictures.

This same photographer is usually my choice for an assignment partner. Howard and I work well together. We know, without having to spell out the situation, which one of us should be in the foreground. We know each other's rhythms and techniques. When we were doing a story on actress Susan Dey for *Look* magazine and found her reluctant to talk about herself, Howard was able to make her relax and soon she was helping me fill my notebook with one good quote after another. In a piece we did for *Saturday Review* on the closing of reform schools in Massachusetts, I was able to talk security officers into letting Howard take photographs of the solitary confinement cages.

It's not necessary to work with a photographer friend, but it helps. It keeps you from making mistakes like this one, which I've heard more than once:

"Hello, I'm Joe Doaks and I'm here to write a profile of you for *Beautiful British Columbia Magazine*. They think you'd make a wonderful subject. . . .Oh, who's this fellow? He's my photographer."

That implication of ownership suggests that the photographer is lowly; that his contribution to the story is less important than the words. And that just isn't true, even if we writers wish it were. Subscribers and newsstand buyers don't read regional magazines first—they *look* at them. If the photographs or other illustrations seem tempting, they will take a bite of the prose. If the photographer was doing the introductions and said ". . .Oh, who's this fellow: He's my writer," he'd be much closer to the truth.

But let's assume that if you were introducing the photographer, you would actually be introducing yourself. You're a writer *and* a photographer. Well, I'm an editor and there are a few things I'd like to say to you—you of the multiple talents.

First, don't be thin-skinned. I might give you a dual assignment on the strength of what I know about one of your skills and be very disappointed in the other. One writer who contributes to *Vermont Life* from time to time always wants to provide his own photographs. And his photographs are always mediocre. They are not awful or dreadful—which would make the problem quite solvable. They are mediocre; a touch out of focus or of a composition which isn't quite right or lighting that's just a shade off.

On the other hand, this writer's words are seldom less than superb. He's a heck of a writer and an average photographer. *Vermont Life* doesn't publish average photographs—that's been a policy for decades (and will be for decades to come). But really good writers are rare or at least rare enough to make me want to stay on good terms with those who contribute to the magazine I edit. So when this fellow suggests a story idea the conversation goes like this:

"Vachon, I've got a great story idea for you."

"I'm delighted. Write me a note about it."

"No time, no time. I need a go-ahead today."

"Paul, you know I like written queries. What could be so urgent?"

"A thirty-inch snowstorm."

"You're right. That might have a touch of urgency to it.

When's this supposed to happen?"

"Tonight."

"Tonight?"

"Yea. Heard it on the radio. Best blizzard of the year. One hundred percent chance of snow—two and a half feet of it. Super blizzard!"

" 'Super' and 'best' are not words I normally associate with blizzards. What's your story?"

"Well, I'll go to Chelsea—town of about 200—right? And I'll spend the night there. Got friends who'll put me up. Tomorrow morning, I'll go out and watch Chelsea dig out of two and a half feet of snow. Do the kids make it to school? Do the stores open? Do shut-ins get visited to make sure they have enough goods and fuel? Do neighbors help each other plow driveways? It's a terrific story."

And it was. A lovely idea, just right for Vermont Life, and I know Paul will write it beautifully and that it will be a major feature in next winter's issue. Because of the pressing nature of the situation (and against all my wiser instincts), I gave Paul the photo assignment as well as writing assignment. The idea was a good one and I would never assign it to someone else after hearing it from him. Most editors are pretty conscientious about not doing things like that.

That night, indeed, thirty inches of snow blanketed most of Vermont. Three weeks later, Paul was in my office with a one-thousand word piece that was filled with warmth, good humor, and brightly delivered anecdotes and quotes. Just what I knew he was capable of. And the photographs? Also what I knew he was capable of. Not good. Not bad. Not publishable by Vermont Life.

I waited for another blizzard so that I could send a real photographer to back up Paul's splendid words. Naturally, we didn't get another one. First winter in memory that Vermont had only one blizzard. So the story had to be put on the shelf for an entire year. You never get a blizzard when you want one.

I had sent a writer out to do a photographer's job, and that was my mistake. His lenses were wrong or his f-stops were off or he didn't know how to use a tripod or filters or maybe his hands were shaky. It doesn't matter. He failed to produce and so we failed to produce a check for his written efforts. I couldn't pay for a story that was only half done.

Never jeopardize your words for a lack of pictures. Paul lost out because we didn't have another blizzard. The same problem might be repeated during *any* snowstorm in Hawaii, hurricane in New Hampshire, or drought in Oregon. Timing is essential. Good photographers know how to seize rare moments.

They also know and respect Murphy's Law.

I've heard half a dozen explanations of the origins of that law. This is the one I like best: In 1915, a guy named Murphy bought an automobile and drove it to Ohio where he had a collision with another automobile—the only other car in the state. Murphy's Law: If something can go wrong, it will.

For photographers, that law covers running out of film as the sun breaks from behind the clouds; shooting the most dazzling rainbow since Noah bumped his ark into a mountain—with the lens cap on; shooting six rolls of film of a rodeo in Wyoming and then finding out your ASA setting was three stops off; or leaving your film in a conventional suitcase and allowing it to pass beneath an X-ray scanner at the airport. Photographers get used to the bitter truth of Murphy's Law.

At *Vermont Life*, the Law hit home in a particularly painful way when two thousand color slides were mistaken for trash by the night janitor and hauled to the dump. The staff spent three hours the next day clawing through week-old fish, mountains of used kitty litter and things I don't even want to write about. We recovered most of the slides, but about two hundred were gone forever. The accident was no one's fault: the janitor wasn't being malicious; no one at *Vermont Life* had been derelict in his duties; the owner of the landfill couldn't be blamed for having a particularly pungent pile of throw-outables that morning. It was just one of those things.

One of those awful, Murphy things. *

But photographers can take precautions to keep Murphy-isms at a minimum.

First, if you see a good picture, shoot it twice. Ed Mahanna of Lenox, Massachusetts, has been taking pictures for more than fifty years. When he sees a scene he likes, he might shoot it ten times. He brackets to make certain he's got exactly the right exposure. And he might alter the angle here and there. But basically, he believes there is no such thing as too much of a beautiful thing.

More and more photographers are having the labs make duplicate transparencies and sending only the duplicates to editors. We don't mind that, if we know we can have access to the originals when we want them.

Smart photographers who fly don't "carry-on" their film. They leave it with the luggage that is not X-rayed.

Photographers can also help themselves by finding out what regional magazine editors are specifically looking for.

* (Several photographers who lost their slides suggested they would sue but I urged them not to, and I wasn't merely being self-protective. The photographs that had been lost had not been solicited. *Vermont Life* had no liability because we hadn't asked for them. A suit would be good for the lawyers and no one else. "On the other hand," I told the photographers "I feel an obligation to you that I won't forget. The next idea you present is going to get a long study before it's rejected, if it's rejected."

Finally I told the grieving photographers something that is unfortunately true. *Every* magazine has one major disaster. It is absolutely inevitable. After the disaster happens, the system of recording photographs gets changed, security is tightened and the staff heaves a sigh of relief. "It's behind us now," I told the staff in our case. "The big one is over. We don't have to worry about sending slides to the dump again. We've done it."

The photographers didn't sue, and we never lost another slide.)

At *Vermont Life* we like color transparencies to be 35 millimeter or 2¼-inch square, and we like them sent in plastic slide holders. We generally like to see black and white on contact sheets before prints are made up; that saves the photographer some guesswork on what we're looking for. We can't work from color prints. And we react to tiny photographs wrapped up in giant wads of tissue paper with an involuntary but very noticeable shudder.

I want photographers to edit their slides carefully and send me only ones that they would want to see published. But the edited slides should not be so picked over that the art director and I are left with none to pass on. I want to have some choices.

Clyde Smith, one of the nation's leading photographers for regional magazines, always sends me no fewer than forty slides for every assignment. Sometimes as many as eighty. But he knows that more than that will bother me. I'll get itchy about looking at eighty-two pictures of the same situation.

Some photographers—and forgive me, but this is true—who are quite good and also happen to be female have a tendency to send me finished mounted black and white prints that they have labored over in their darkrooms. Why that seems to be a feminine trait I will never know. But I'm not looking for finished mounted black and white prints that may or may not accompany a story. That's too much trouble up front.

I'm also turned off by photographers who send me complicated forms assigning me first rights and telling me how much I will have to compensate them if their work gets lost (I tell those photographers to get lost). I'd rather work with the Clyde Smiths of this world.

Other magazines might have other desires and biases. Nearly every regional magazine has a specifications sheet for photographers, and editors send them upon request. If the request comes enclosed with a self-addressed stamped envelope, we will have a positive memory of the requestor. We feel warmly inclined toward people who save us postage.

Photographers or writer-photographers should study the magazine they are submitting to very closely and get familiar with the art director's style. What kind of pictures are being blown up and shown dramatically? What sort of stories are being presented in color and which run black and white? Does the art director have a tendency to crop photographs? (That question was rhetorical. *All* art directors crop photographs and photographers who complain that their work is being ruined, that a full frame means a *full frame*, are prima donnas most editors and art directors can do nicely without.)

Vermont Life, for example, seldom shows interiors in color. The lighting is bad and since the magazine has 64 pages but only 32 pages of color capacity, I'll make certain our story on life inside a Carthusian monastery is black and white. The editor of *New Jersey* magazine uses very little color, and I'm not certain what implication can be drawn from that.

What are the taboos in the magazine you are submitting to? My predecessor at *Vermont Life* hated showing telephone lines and only relented when it became obvious that photographers would have to become contortionists to shoot around them. My taboos include hunting pictures (I have nothing against hunting, but the magazine's audience does, for the most part) and flower close-ups (you can't see Vermont in a close-up of a dandelion). I am not interested in photographs taken of the sky through a blazing mosaic of leaves or photographs of dew on a spider's web. (I've seen more dew on spider webs than any insect buff you can name.)

Most regionals aren't interested in photographs depicting poverty, crime, moral or physical decay, or politicians. The magazines are looking for pictures that show the *region* off—its best points, its highlights. We like to pictorially brag about our regions. Give us pictures which beckon.

Find that interesting angle. A covered bridge picture *will* excite me if it's taken from a vantage point that no photographer has succeeded with before. The Grand Canyon must have nearly an infinite number of places from which photographers can point and shoot. Indiana's cornfields at midday are not likely to interest the editor of *Indiana* any more. But cornfields during an electric storm might.

Most regional magazines that feature color photographs have sections that are purely scenic. *Vermont Life* reserves eight pages an issue to seasonal color photographs that show off Vermont. I find myself looking, four times a year, at photographs that aren't attached to any particular story but that send the Vermont message. If the regional that you are interested in is similarly inclined, find out when the editor is looking for what, and fill his needs. (It does no good to send early. If I want fall scenics in May, which is when I want them, you won't score any points by sending me dazzling foliage in March. In fact it will put you on the bottom of the pile.)

We editors are also on the lookout for good illustrations. All regional magazines use some form of non-photographic illustration. *Vermont Life* favors pen and ink drawings when we can't offer photographs. *Arizona Highways* and *Georgia Life* have always favored watercolor and oil paintings. The city slicks generally go for black and white caricatures and weekly newspaper supplements favor cartoons. Find out what your intended recipient has gone with, and you'll know immediately what it wants. *Vermont Life* will almost never reproduce an oil painting, and one look at our last ten issues will drive that point home. (We printed one: it was by Norman Rockwell and we didn't even bother to put it on a color page. See how devoted to photography we are?)

If the magazine you are working for likes painting—like *Omni*, the magazine whose region is the universe—have your piece accompanied by something dazzling and original.

Few regional magazines are interested in abstract or conceptual art. The decoration that accompanies most pieces should be realistic and faithful to the regions they are depicting. "When I show a painting of Wisconsin," says

Howard Mead, publisher of *Wisconsin Trails*, "I want that painting to look like Wisconsin. Not Minnesota or Iowa, but Wisconsin. That's the place we're showing off."

Painters who aren't exceptional should leave their hobby at home. Don't put editors on the spot. I always feel more than a little awkward when a would-be artist shows me his work. I'm not an art critic. I don't know impressionism from expressionism from cubism. I do know Vermont and what our readers want to see in the state magazine. They don't want to see someone else's impressions (though it could be deftly argued that a slick, straightforward color scenic photograph is someone else's impression). They want to see Vermont. Green mountains. Covered bridges. Old farm houses. Don't put me on the spot with a water color and acrylic collage of a fantasy waterfall. I won't understand it. Or like it. And I'll probably tell you so.

But where do you find a good polished artist, assuming that you are not an artist of that variety yourself? What if the editor wants some drawings with your piece and has delegated the responsibility of finding those drawings to you?

There are a number of places to look. Most advertising agencies worth their salt employ someone who is deft with art, layout, and design (and who might enjoy working on something "less commercial"). Or you might try a nearby college and ask to speak to an outstanding art student. That student will be so hungry for the exposure the fact that there will be a fee involved will come as a surprise. And remember, you don't have to pay the fee. Writers don't pay photographers or illustrators: magazines do.

Don't get your son-in-law to accompany your article with illustrations unless your son-in-law is *really* good. A nice rule of thumb is, has he had at least two one-man shows in galleries located in cities with more than one hundred thousand residents? If so, he'll do fine. If not, be careful. It's not that I have anything against your son-in-law. It's just that I would hate to see you lose a very nice writing assignment just because your daughter married a fellow who thinks he's an artist.

When in Vermont
(or Atlanta ... or Dallas)

Strategies for freelance survival

Like most other writers, I encounter situations in which my creative flow ebbs, and even ceases to exist. One of these is trying to do freelance writing in my home, wherever that home might be. I couldn't write in my one-story ranch house in San Diego or my brownstone apartment in Manhattan, and I can't write at my home in Vermont, surrounded by woods, singing birds, and an occasional white-tailed deer. (Though one would think it is the perfect environment to write for *Vermont Life*.)

This is not a complaint: it's an observation. I've not checked it out with psychological authorities, but my uneducated guess is that my system is telling me home is where I'm to relax, be with my family, unwind. I can't do any of those things when I'm writing, and so I have made it a practice not to write at home. I borrow an office, or rent one. I leave the tranquillity of the place in which I live (which is not *always* tranquil but is most of the time) and go elsewhere for my typewriter time.

I offer that observation because I've heard some perfectly capable writers tell me they feel it's impossible to accomplish anything. When I ask where they are working, they say they have fashioned a little den in their basements or have turned the guest bedroom into an office. But they can't get anything done. Try getting out of the house and see if things loosen up. Your writer's block might just be powerfully distracting surroundings.

Usually that piece of advice works. When a writer finds an environment that is free of "off-time" associations, he begins to write.

But even in a perfect writing environment you may encounter blocks.

Such as the nemesis we all talk about and dread—the paralysis of all writing ability. Our minds turn to mush and the blank paper in the typewriter seems to be mocking us. It happens to everyone. Margaret Mitchell started writing *Gone With the Wind* when she was 25 years old and tidied up the final chapter ten years later. Sure, it was a fine and lengthy novel but it wasn't *that* fine and lengthy.

Isaac Asimov, the science fiction genius who turns out prose faster than most of us mortals can *think*, may not block, but Ronald Rood—who has authored a dozen nature books and many dozen regional magazine articles—does. When it hits, he goes to the kitchen and makes himself a sandwich. Would that it were so easy for all of us.

When your blocks come, the first thing you should give yourself is a dose of analysis. Have you stopped writing because you're really not interested in or excited by the subject? That's certainly a legitimate reason. But if the piece I'm writing has been committed—if I'm working on assignment and have promised to come up with the goods—a lack of stimulation won't justify abandoning the project. I have a reputation for being dependable and I want to keep it. Thus my "Gritting-the-Teeth Block Buster." I force myself—I pull my chair up to the typewriter, surround myself with the proper tools and research, and I start writing.

If the lead is flabby, I'll whip out that piece of paper and roll in a new one. If my first twenty-three leads lack pizzazz, I'll start on a twenty-fourth. Eventually, something clicks, and when the lead is right, the rest seems to fall reasonably and easily into place.

Have you ever heard someone say they had something to tell you but didn't know how to begin? Whenever I hear someone prelude bad news that way (it's always bad news) I say, "Well, you've already begun so let's get on with it."

Not knowing how to begin a magazine article—or a book or a college essay, for that matter—is common. But sometimes the best way to start is to plunge right in. Bull it through.

An example of a forced lead that worked is this one written for a *Playboy* piece on crying and the fact that men don't do it enough. I loved the subject, believed firmly in the premise, but couldn't figure out how I could seriously address the subject of male weeping in a magazine that aims at stirring opposite emotions. Finally, after many tries, sandwiches, walks around the block, and a few good cries myself, I came up with this:

> Midway through my freshman year of college, I received a Dear John letter from a young woman whom I professed to love demonstrably more than my own life. It was quite a letter. Her words—written with superb spareness—hurt me more than I had ever been hurt before. And so I reacted to the hurt in a way in which I think many members of my gender react when faced with a situation of inconsolable grief. I walked down to my dormitory bathroom and vomited into the sink.

That lead carried enough strength to propel me through the rest of the article where I talked about the fact that men don't cry when they should. It also provided the comedy/pathos dichotomy that was just right for *Playboy*'s general style.

Let me emphasize again, that lead didn't fall out of my fertile imagination and into type. It was wrenched out. It got written only after I agonized for more than a little while. But it did get written.

Murder can be a tough subject for anyone to write about, and when Mike Mallowe had a moment of trouble getting started on a book review for *Philadelphia* (which *loves* crime pieces) he decided to just bull it through. Start smack in the beginning and go like hell.

> The man who owns the Dorchester, David Marshall, says the murder was no reflection on his security system. "We can't police who goes into the apartments and what goes on inside them," he explained, referring to that grisley morning exactly three years ago when John Knight III was hacked to death in his $1,050-a-month apartment. . . .

From there, Mallowe reviewed the book "Kings Don't Mean a Thing" and the murder of Knight—a millionaire, homosexual playboy—and the subsequent investigation, suspicions, hypothesis, and motives. There are times the writer must grit his teeth, square his shoulders, and plunge ahead.

Sometimes we writers crash into a block because something is distracting us. Such as when I find myself fading out halfway through a modest declarative sentence. I can't think of a synonym for "nice" and I can't think of where to find one. I'm absolutely blocked and words won't come no matter how hard I grit my teeth.

That's a "Distraction Block." Which means I left for my office that morning with my son screaming for no reason and my wife resenting my escape. I feel guilty. Of *course* I can't write. I've got to go home and take my son for a stroll and give my wife a breather. That's all it takes, and I'm ready to start writing again.

If you're blocking and you really can't figure out why, it's probably because something other than the pertinent subject matter is on your mind. And until you discover and resolve that elusive other, the block will remain firmly in place. So search your conscience. Pinpoint the haunting problem. Come up with a solution that will solve or at least temporarily satisfy it and carry it out. Then hopefully you can return with a relatively clear mind to that smirking typewriter and surprise the hell out of it.

Sometimes we block because the subject matter we're writing about is so difficult or so emotional that it just seems impossible to get started. Writer Madeleine Kunin, who later was to become Vermont's Lieutenant Governor, did a piece for *Vermont Life* that had those ingredients. She admitted it was one of the toughest pieces she ever wrote. It had to do with the Foster Grandparent program—one in which elderly persons of limited income are matched-up with severely retarded youngsters for intense, one-on-one fellowship and therapy. The program is superb, the subject was perfect for the magazine, but how could she get started? After many false starts, this is what Kunin came up with:

> "Give Grandma a smile. Have you a smile for Grandma today?" The white-haired woman in the pink smock leaned over the large iron crib and stroked the child's pale forehead. Slowly, her impassive face registered Grandma's voice. "Come give us a smile," the voice coaxed. With visible effort, the child reached out from her limited world. A smile appeared and the transformation was as dramatic as if she had thrown off a mask. Another victory. Pam knows Grandma.

Kunin used some pretty ordinary adjectives—"white-haired woman," "large iron crib," "child's pale forehead." But did she get the desired results? You'd better believe it. That difficult story sang for 2,000 words because the first 79 words set the mood.

Sometimes we block because we're tired. That's an easy one to overcome: take a nap.

One nap—not two or three or four (or you end up in another block—the sleep-escape block).

Sometimes I block on a magazine article because I'm not in the mood. Sorry for being that imprecise, but that's the problem. Not tired, not distracted, not facing a difficult writing situation—just not in the mood.

That's the best time to write query letters, or at least it's the best time for me to write them. Because editing *Vermont Life* is a fulltime job, my freelance writing has to be accomplished on weekends and evenings. I've set Saturday afternoon as my time for putting words on paper to improve the family income. Saturday afternoon is when that has to happen. No excuses.

But what happens if I'm not in the mood on a particular Saturday afternoon? What if I have three good assignments thoroughly researched and ready to roll but I just don't feel like writing them?

Well, I *could* make a last-minute change in my schedule, decide to set Sunday afternoon aside instead, and hope my mood will be more productive the next day. But that's sloppy. We freelance writers are supposed to be a little more disciplined than that.

And so I take those not-in-the-mood Saturday afternoons and put them to another use. You don't have to be in a special mood to write query letters. Exalted, humbled, enervated, energized—it doesn't make a bit of difference. Query letters are mechanical operations. They should be done skillfully— in order to produce the required results—but there's a formula and once you know the formula, you should be able to write query letters that work even if you're in no mood to write at all. It all goes back to turning an editor on, making him sit up and take notice.

The formula goes like this:

Get the name, proper title, and address of the editor to whom the query is being directed.

Determine the date.

Put the date on the upper right-hand corner of a plain piece of white paper and the name, title, and address of your editor on the left.

Give the editor a semi-formal salutation.

Write an enticing lead (with a hook, a twist, or something that gives it impact).

Then write a billboard paragraph (see Chapter Four) explaining precisely what article you would like to write, how long it will run, how it might best be decorated, and how soon you can have it completed.

Write a third paragraph expanding on the second if you feel that is necessary.

Write a fourth paragraph explaining the reasons why you are the perfect person to write this particular piece. Mention a few credentials and past accomplishments if you have any. (If you won a Pulitzer, for example, it could do no harm to let that fact slip out. If you've never published a word in any form except for an angry letter to the editor of your local newspaper expressing your views on gay rights, don't bother getting into accomplishments.)

Write a complimentary close. "Sincerely," "Regards," and "Yours Truly" are all perfectly acceptable. "Peace," "Have A Nice Day," and "Keep Up the Good Work" are not.

And there, you've written a query. I make certain I write at least one query every week.

Of course now there's the possibility that you may receive a rejection slip rather than an assignment call in response to your query. I send 52 story ideas out to magazine editors each year. If my batting average were .1000 I'd have to quit my job, but I'm batting closer to .250 and that allows me to remain both an editor and a freelance writer. About one out of every four of my queries gets a favorable response. The other three out of four get rejections. Every year, I get about thirty-nine rejection slips. I can bear them.

Some people can't. There are some folks who get absolutely apoplectic whenever an editor suggests that the story idea he or she has submitted isn't quite right for that particular magazine. And that's an awful waste of energy. There's nothing wrong with rejection slips: they just come in varying degrees of courteous disinterest.

Most regional magazines are willing to respond personally to a thoughtful query letter—even when that response is negative. When the editor of *The Carolina Sportman* turns down a monograph on bobwhite quail, it's probably because interest in quail has slackened in recent seasons. But he might tell you he is interested, among other things, in confession stories with an outdoor setting. Or so he said to the editors of *Writer's Market*.

Once when I was in high school, I sent a batch of poetry to a small pretentious literary magazine. The poetry, or so I thought then, bordered on the immortal. The rejection slip, conversely, was decidedly temporal. "Sorry" someone has scrawled on a scrap of paper. My poems were not returned, nor was there any indication of their worth or the degree of my correspondents' regrets. "Sorry" was all she or he wrote.

(Two parenthetical asides. First, there was no compelling reason why those poems *should* have been returned. The little magazine had not solicited them and I had failed to enclose a stamped, self-addressed envelope. Second, I do have to admit *that* rejection slip wounded me somewhat. When I learned a year later that the little magazine folded for lack of supporting capital, I felt a pleasing surge of inner warmth.)

The toughest rejection slip I ever got went like this:

Dear Mr. Vachon:
  Our Planning Council turned down your idea for an article on the Franco-Americans—this, despite my support.
  Thank you for submitting the suggestion. Please try us again.

The letter was signed by the director of photography of *National Geographic*—the world's most successful regional magazine. It hurt me to my normally well-insulated quick because I had put a great deal of labor and research into the query. I shouldn't have—the mistake was mine. I should have tested the water with my toe, not my torso. But it was too late. A photographer and I had put together an enormous and rich portfolio and story summary and presented it, without a word of prior encouragement or interest, to that Washington-based magazine. Despite that presumptuous and ignorant action on our part, the director of photography evidently liked what he saw. (His feelings obviously did not affect the Planning Council's decision.)

That's the last time I'll ever spend a two-week vacation researching a query letter. I now try to limit myself to ten minutes, and that includes the time it takes to make a copy of the original. (Always make copies of your queries so that when an editor says "Yes," you'll have evidence of what he is agreeing to.)

One magazine to which this advice doesn't apply is *Writer's Digest*, where editor John Brady replies "Yes" or "No" or gives editorial maybes in the margin or on the back of the letter, and ships the query right back to the sender. He affixes a rubber stamp explanation: "To conserve our national forests—the reply to your letter has been written on your letter." I'd do that at *Vermont Life* if I had his nerve (we probably have more forests, anyway).

The rejection slip showing the most discernible degree of disinterest is the one that has been printed. Mine goes like this:

Dear Contributor:
   Thank you for letting us see your manuscript.
   I'm afraid we are in a situation right now where we are buying virtually no new material until our rather substantial editorial backlog is published.
   At that time—perhaps within a year—we will again be actively soliciting new material and hope you will think of us again.

                              Regards,
                              Brian Vachon
                              Editor

Clearly that was a rejection slip written by someone who *receives* rejection slips. Me. That preprinted piece of prevarication* was meant to say "No" in the nicest possible way to a would-be contributor. I really don't like hurting any writer's feelings. The times I come closest to doing that occur when I've received a manuscript or query that just misses being terrific in an obvious and conspicuous way. A manuscript that profiles a terribly fascinating person, for example, but never bothers to quote him. Or a query that proposes a story on skinny dipping but refrains from saying where that practice might go on (or come off). That irritates me and my rejection slip will be written in such a way that there is no doubt in the writer's mind that he has irritated me. Total failures find me generous though discouraging. Middling failures find me helpful and assuring. Near misses made me mad.

I reserve my printed rejection slip for those writers whose writing is so bad or whose subject matter is so out of touch with what I'm looking for or whose manuscript is so illegible that I have to refuse to take the two minutes necessary to write a personal note. These folks get the pink slip. So do writers who send me Xeroxed or carboned copies of their work. If I can't be privy to original copy, I'm immediately underwhelmed.

I should quickly add here that all editors don't have the time or inclination to create individualized rejection slips. I do—and I enjoy writing them, but that just may be a personal editorial deviation. I love getting a manuscript or query letter from someone I've never heard of, containing an idea that just might be right for *Vermont Life*. I write that person back immediately, telling him or her how the idea can be honed and shaped and tuned so that it will really work for the magazine. I send letters like that every day and they make me feel as if I'm conducting a major literary symphony spread all over the United States and eastern Canada.

* Look it up. I was looking for a word which meant "untruth" and which started with a "p" so that I could slip a little alliteration in on you. I got the word from my *Synonym Finder* and I instantly fell in love with it. I will undoubtedly use "prevarication" again.

If you receive an individualized rejection slip, from me or any other editor who composes one, learn to read between the lines. If you get a scrap of paper that says "Sorry," there aren't many lines to read between. But you might also get a rejection that says:

Thanks for your suggestion on doing a piece on dog racing in northern Maine. I'm afraid, though, that we recently did a long section of various Maine dogs and we now probably should stay away from the puppies for a while. But thanks.

Now that's a nice rejection slip. That editor wouldn't mind seeing another query from you tomorrow.

If you write to Geoff Miller, the editor of *Los Angeles*, and said you were a friend of Brooke Shields's mother and wanted to do a story about her, you might get this reply:

Thanks for the query on Brooke Shields. We agree with you: it's about time the people of Los Angeles get to know more about this child star—more about who she is and not what she looks like. In fact we agree with you so much that we commissioned a story on Brooke last month.

Sorry you were a little late on this one. But keep the ideas coming.

That is rejection of the very nicest sort.

I received this rejection slip from a Maritime Province magazine:

Thanks for writing last month and I apologize for not getting back to you sooner. But you were right when you expressed the fear that we wouldn't want another "East Coast's largest lobster" article at the moment. Why don't you send along some other ideas, though. We'd love to have you represented in the magazine.

How much time do you think elapsed between the moment I read that utterly charming rejection slip and the time I had another query in the mail to the same editor? Not much.

Read your rejection slips prudently. Make sure you know what has been said and what has been implied. Don't take "no" for an answer when "please try again: you've raised our interest" was the intended message.

The intended message of this chapter was that writing doesn't *have* to be difficult. Since we are all filled with foibles, we routinely heave difficulties out of the bushes and plunk them in our path. And then we say, "Oh my God, look at that terrible difficulty. It's right in my path. I guess I can't write today." And we don't write that day.

But if we kept the difficulties where they belong—out of sight and mind—writing would be as easy for any reasonably intelligent, articulate person as talking is. Have you ever heard anyone say they had talker's block? Not when they were involved in a short conversation. Writing magazine articles is the literary equivalent of having a short but clever conversation.

Did you ever know anyone who stopped talking because one listener said he wasn't interested in the words?

You'd think a person that easily intimidated was running around with some pretty questionable emotional baggage. Yet there are many writers who can't face their typewriters after receiving a single rejection slip. They've taken a very small setback and made it a difficulty around which they cannot get.

Silliness.

Writing is talking. People who are reasonably articulate can write. If they let themselves go. Foreward.

Sunny Side Up

Writing for positive publications

I'm the editor of a positive publication. I used to apologize for that fact or get defensive about it. The critics who told me positive publications like *Vermont Life* have no business being in business were getting to me. Maybe they were right, I thought.

And then I thought again.

To state it in the simplest possible terms, magazines like the one I edit make people happy—or nostalgic or visionary—and that's their purpose. As long as positive publications tell the truth about their regions, they serve a very real function. These publications are *needed*. People love to read them. They confirm hopes and dreams. "Is there really a place on earth that is still that way?" The answer in positive publications is a resounding shout. "Yes. Right *here*." And even if that glorious reality being proclaimed is an illusion of sorts (and I argue that it is not) who among us does not need illusions? A routine complaint about the magazine I edit is that we don't tell the *whole* truth. Well, that's true. We don't. Nor does any newspaper, magazine, television news, or radio show tell the whole truth. There isn't time, space, or (for the most part) interest. And so there has to be some picking and choosing. Most media choose to tell the bad news and that's what pays their bills. Positive regionals tell the good news (and that pays ours). Which half of the story would you rather get if you were limited to only one? Or more to the point, isn't it fine that no such limitation is placed upon you?

And that's one reason why resourceful freelancers should itch to write for them. Nothing is more satisfying to a writer—or at least to this particular writer—than to have written something that readers appreciate. That means more to me than a check I receive, and that's a fact. I like the check a whole lot, but I like being appreciated by an audience even more.

I want you to share those good feelings.

Positive publications are everywhere. Every state has at least one, the provinces of Canada have many, lots of counties have one, and some towns even do. Positive publications will never die. Just think of all those opportunities to be appreciated.

The differences between positive publications are these: Some may be owned by the state or county or province which they extol, while others may be owned by chambers of commerce or even privately owned. State-owned magazines are far less likely to criticize their regions than private publications. Chamber of commerce publications never criticize *anything*.

Positive publications also differ in that some may be geared strictly to residents of their region and others may be geared to nonresidents. Ninety percent of *Vermont Life*'s readers don't live in Vermont. The same is true of the readers of *Arizona Highways*. Eighty percent of *Alaska*'s 200,000 subscribers reside in the lower forty-eight. On the other hand, about half the readers of *Down East* "The Magazine of Maine" live in Maine, and an even higher percentage of *Blue*

Nose Rambler readers live in Downeast Canada. It's important to find out what the readership is, just because it's good to know who you're talking to. There's no Vermonter alive who doesn't know that Mount Mansfield is the state's largest peak. But because my readers are non-Vermonters, I do not assume they know that fact. Stories that mention Mount Mansfield also mention its height and distinction.

If you have any questions about the make-up of the readership of the positive publication you want to write for, call the editorial office and ask. We editors are glad to tell you writers as much as we can: it ultimately makes our jobs easier.

I've mentioned the differences in positive publications. I will now dwell ever-so-briefly on the obvious and mention what makes them all similar. They are all positive. They all have a bright and cheery outlook. They survey their regions through the front door. "We attempt to examine Illinois from an open-eyed perspective," says Daniel Malkovitch, editor and publisher of *Illinois* magazine. "We're not seeking warts but not hiding those that appear."

The United States' most famous positive magazine is *Arizona Highways*, which has earned its three-quarters of a million circulation and reputation for excellence by being consistently superb in theme and photography. Of the regionals in the private sector, *Sunset* reigns in the West and *Southern Living* in the South. *Yankee* is king in New England and *Blair and Ketchum's Country Journal* has made "the country" their region. *Metro*, the magazine of southeastern Virginia; *Maryland*, about the state of the same name; and *Missouri Life* each have nonexclusive bragging rights to their particular territories. It's all a matter of editorial ambition and readership demand.

Vermont Life has over 100,000 subscribers and a reputation built over thirty years for outstanding color photography. That's our bread and butter—beautiful pictures. People look at our green mountains, running rivers, and covered bridges and they are guilty of territorial lust. They hunger for Vermont.

And that's fine. But I'm also a word man, and I want my readers to *read* about Vermont. That's why I look for the best writers I can find and why we're willing to pay to up $500 for intelligently or humorously or informatively written articles. Most of the articles are assigned to freelancers. The rest are assigned to me. Most other positive publications have about the same ratio—nine out of ten stories and story ideas come from the outside. Whether the positive magazine you're thinking about writing for is a weekly, a monthly, or a quarterly, the editor usually has his or her hands full without having the additional responsibility of originating every idea for every article published. We all need help from freelancers.

Let's make it a fair exchange. I'll offer you some advice on writing for positive publications. Ten good rules:

One: Know the region you're writing about. You can't write about Oklahoma if you've never been outside Boston. But you'd be amazed at how many people try. At *Vermont Life*, we regularly get articles about life in Vermont as writers imagine it in Florida or theorize it in Nevada. To publish writing from such vantage points, even if it is brilliant (and sometimes it is) would be to defeat our purpose. People read positive regionals because they want to know about that particular region. They have a proprietary interest. They want to feel part of it. They want to feel a certain sense of pride in sharing knowledge of a special corner of the world they count as their own. Even when they are absentee landlords. They want to share in the glorious conspiracy that is Colorado, or Baja, or Arkansas.

They don't want impressions from obvious outsiders: they want facts and feelings from insiders. (That doesn't mean you necessarily have to live in North Carolina to write about North Carolina. It just means the Tarheel State and you have to be on pretty close terms if you plan to submit something to *North Carolina Magazine*.)

You might be writing the account of your Oregon fishing trip in Illinois, but your memory of that fishing trip in Eugene had better be mighty clear. Your notes had better be voluminous.

Two: Being positive doesn't mean pushing. Positive magazines do promote their regions, but their editors generally would rather not appear to be blatantly promotional. That may not have been true back in the early 1900s when almost all regionals took the form of chamber of commerce publications and sold their regions with unmitigated gusto. Even as late as 1968, Vermont billed itself as "the beckoning country" and beckon it did, with promotional literature of every sort. Most of that literature was distributed free to the public. *Vermont Life* was sold but it was also subsidized by the state. But times have changed. My magazine no longer gets a legislative appropriation. We have to support ourselves. And Vermont no longer calls itself the beckoning country. We're backing off that position, mostly because it was a little bit *too* successful. If Vermont is to continue to be attractive, it has to continue to be rural. That's Vermont's charm. If too many people got beckoned up here, our ruralness would be gone.

Other states are putting the brakes on their open invitations to lesser degrees. Colorado and Maine are feeling they want folks to come and admire but not come and live. Alabama and North Dakota, on the other hand, are still actively hustling themselves. *New Mexico* magazine, sponsored by the state department of Commerce and Industry and one of the rare government-supported publications that accepts private sector advertising, bills its region as "the heart of the Southwest." Missouri's monthly travel promotion has the tagline, "Missouri loves company."

But regardless of whether the appeal is subtle or blatant, the positive publications are positive. They still want to show you the best about the regions they cover, but not obsequiously. The photography can be inoffensively promotional but the writing should not be. It should be literate.

Don't talk too much about the Duponts in *Delaware* magazine or the Cabots and Lodges in *Boston*. Don't get carried away by the people and places of the region you are presenting: just wave the flag a bit. Soft sell always works better than hard in writing. As soon as a positive magazine starts blatantly hawking its product—its region—that magazine loses credibility. After credibility falleth the readership. Sometimes the line between writing positively and writing promotionally is a thin one. But writers—you—only need to remember to present some aspect or feature or personality of a region that will make the readership feel positive about that particular territory. You don't have to gloss over a region's blemishes or avoid controversy at all cost, but the writing in a positive publication has to give pleasure. We positive publication editors are in the pleasure business. I get letters every day from people who tell me what a good job I'm doing. So do other regional magazine editors. But those letters aren't really judging the strength of our performance. They're responding to the appeal of our particular region.

Three: Make the lead paragraph absolutely sing. Make the editor really pay attention with a lead that has strength and color and character. This is true for any magazine market but especially true for positive publications because their editors don't have time to read through weak prose. There are too many potentially strong manuscripts waiting on our desks. Plenty of writers out there would like to see their by-lines in our pages. On a normal morning, I might get a dozen unsolicited manuscripts along with queries, complaints, compliments, and questions in my mail. Between my secretary and myself, we have to deal with all of that and because there are only two of us, our dealings are sometimes cursory. I don't know if I'd read every manuscript sent here even if I had the time. But since I definitely do *not* have the time, I read the leads. If they spark my interest, I'll read on. If the first few paragraphs are dull and listless, I'll skim on quickly—to see if there's anything worth salvaging—and then I return to sender with a very short note. Writers might not know that editors treat them that way, but they invite it with dull leads.

Four: Query first. Positive publications always read queries carefully and completely. Queries tell the editor that the writer has an idea and wants encouragement to pursue it. The editor can then tell the writer that the idea is a good one, and make an assignment right on the spot. Or the editor can tell the writer that the idea is already in the works, or that it has been done recently, or that it is inappropriate. Or, the editor can say he'd like to see the idea developed on a speculation basis. No matter which way it comes out, queries save time. When they are smartly presented, they impress editors.

Five: Make certain your subject is indigenous and even unique to the area. Positive publications want to show off their uniqueness and often dwell on what they have that most other places don't. At *Vermont Life*, I am specifically uninterested in stories about Vermont cattle ranches, although there are several in the state. Next to those in Texas, Vermont cattle ranches look like small backyards. I *am* interested in an article about a one-room schoolhouse that is alive and well, or a town meeting where a group of residents decided to paint the church themselves rather than raise taxes. Those stories have Vermont flavor.

Conversely, "The Vermont Hot Tub Explosion" gets a fast "thanks but no thanks" from me. In a state that endures at least six months of winter, hot tubs simply aren't the rage. Saunas aren't very popular in Louisiana nor indoor pools in the Bahamas. When writers pick the subject first and the region second, it shows. We editors spot that mistake every time.

If you look at a copy of *Arizona Highways*, you most likely will see a photograph of desert vistas. That's something Arizona has that Vermont doesn't. (The former dean of the U.S. Senate, Vermont's George D. Aiken once addressed himself to that fact on the floor during a Senate debate. Arizona's Senator Barry Goldwater had just said something mildly unflattering about *Vermont Life*—with no malice but in order to make a point. Senator Aiken immediately rose to his feet and said: "My colleague from Arizona has a nice little magazine in his state. But the problem with it is, one month all you'll see is sagebrush, cactus and the Grand Canyon, and the next month you'll only see the Grand Canyon, cactus and sagebrush.")

Six: Avoid clichés. Avoid them at all cost because if you don't, they will deprive you of all monetary benefits of freelance writing. This piece of advice is applicable to all writing of any kind but perhaps no place more so than in writing for positive publications. The phrases "rolling hills," "verdant valley," "village nestled in the mountains," and "sparkling spring days" turn me off so quickly, I'm barely able to read another word. References to "Yankee frugality," "independent Vermonters," and "stoic farmers" make me wince. It's not that Vermont doesn't have independent residents or stoic farmers; it's just that those phrases and subjects have been done to death. Even out-of-state readers are tired of regional clichés. Give them new insights. Tell them how to get around and what to see—especially if what you're presenting is unique to the area. Introduce them to the local citizenry, and make them feel welcome. "Uniqueness is conveyed through graphics and writing style," says John Taylor, editor of *Delaware Today*. "All writers are encouraged to be as creative as possible. . . .They [stories] must be written in such a way that someone in California or Iowa could enjoy them, even though the focus is local." Every positive publication editor will quickly tell you his or her collection of overkilled words and descriptions. It's a good idea to read your copy of a freshly written article over with just a cliché search in mind. As you find words that ring a little too familiar, change them.

Seven: Write as if your piece will be unaccompanied by illustration. That is good advice even if the piece will definitely be accompanied by illustration, even photographs that you took yourself. Too many writers use photographs as crutches—as substitutes for creative writing. It is not necessarily repetitious to describe a particular scene and show a photograph of the same scene on the same page of a magazine. That happens all the time in positive publications, and the two coexist and reinforce each other quite nicely. What *does* create a problem is lazy writing. If the writer says the little girl was "pretty" because he knows we'll see a picture of her with her velvet dress and big green eyes, he's cheated me out of a chance to see how vividly he can describe that dress and those eyes. He's opted for weak words because he thinks he can't compete with the mirror image of photography. That kind of surrender gets a writer nowhere fast.

Eight: Don't be afraid of quotes. They almost always brighten up and breathe life into a story. Positive publications are always looking for people who are talking about their subjects in their region. If you're writing about a particular person, let that person come out in his or her own words. There's nothing wrong with a little dialogue either.

> "How long have you been making violins in this little cabin?," I asked the gentleman.
> "Oh, pretty near 60 years," he said without the slightest indication that 60 years was a long time to pursue a single vocation.
> "It seems like you've been making violins all your life," I said.
> "Not yet," he replied evenly, and we exchanged grins.

In a piece on Greenville South Carolina's "Shoeless" Joe Jackson written by James W. Thompson for *Sandlapper*, he recounts this conversation:

> Jackson had found a bundle of money under his hotel pillow before the famous "Black Sox" scandal of 1919, and didn't know where it had come from.
> "More money, I guess, than I'd ever seen in my life in one lump," Joe told me. "Damn," I said. "What did you do then, Joe?"

"I didn't know what to do at first," Joe recalled. "I wanted to cram it down their throats. But I didn't know who 'they' were."

Shoeless Joe was innocent and the point was nicely made in that brief exchange.

Take careful notes when you interview so that you don't misquote. There's nothing at all wrong with saying to an interviewee, "Do you mind repeating that? It's awfully good and I want to make certain I've taken it down right." I do that all the time, and the person I'm interviewing is usually flattered that I care.

Tape recorders are sometimes helpful and they sometimes get in the way. They can catch every word said, giving you time to concentrate on questioning rather than writing. On the other hand, recorders are apt to break down at the most inopportune moments and often make an interviewee nervous. But by whatever method obtained, quotes are *always* helpful in a story. When a region has a human dimension, its appeal improves dramatically.

Nine: Writers for positive publications shouldn't drop names. Names don't generally mean much to most readers of positive publications and they aren't descriptive tools, either. "Mary Smith bid $40 on the old rocking chair" is a phrase that might be found in a story about an auction. But it's not a phrase that tells the reader much of anything. If Mary Smith were described as "tall, guant, seventyish woman with a past—and a future," the reader would be presented with a picture. It's *always* better to show than tell.

Obviously, if you are writing about a specific person, that person should be named. But if you're writing about a country fair, and you fail to identify the four members of the organizational committee, no one will notice but them. And they'll probably get over the slight in a year or so.

Ten: Don't challenge a positive publication's style. Don't try to sell an image or an expression or a point of view that is clearly contrary to the publication's style. That is not to suggest that positive magazines aren't open to change—they are, and do. But changes are made with calculated caution. One of the elements that people love about our magazines is our constancy. They know, for example, that *Vermont Life* is filled with colorful photographs, is relaxed, occasionally nostalgic, and always uses the word "manure" when talking about what farmers have to clean out of barns. They know they will never see a magazine that has gone all black and white, or one that is riled up, or futuristic. And they know "manure" is the only word they'll ever see for manure.

If your aim is a writing assignment don't try to change a positive publication, modernize it, make it more aware, or more relevant. The editors of these magazines are well aware of the style that has been established. Usually is was established long before we arrived on the scene. Our job is to present our region—honestly, but attractively. We are paid to put our region's best face forward, to attract tourists, industry, or just good feelings about our place in the sun. That's what our readers and sponsors want and that's why our magazines were established and why they exist today. If we follow a formula, it's because that formula was tried and found true. You would be wasting your time trying to make us tamper with it.

To summarize those ten tips, be evocative when you are writing for positive publications. Make the reader stand next to you when you are describing a scene, conversation, or event. Use words and phrases and passages that pull your region right off the pages of the magazine you're writing for and plunk it in your reader's living room. Coax your reader into tasting, smelling, and seeing a particular place the way *you* taste and smell and see it. That's what good positive writing is all about.

Need some ideas that might work for practically any positive publication? I might have a few:

1. Find an old house, research its history, find out who lives in it now, and what its future is. Historic preservation is a good idea whose time has finally come.

2. Find an old cemetery and trace the history of one family buried there. Or find out who cuts the lawn and trims the hedges. Cemetery stories don't have to be grim.

3. Do a catalogue of local crafts. What's still being done in your region that isn't being done in any other place in the world? Visit a craft fair. Candlemakers, batik creaters, and macrame-knotters are run of the mill. (That's a pun of significance only in Vermont where the State Craft Center is located in a. . .oh, you know.) But how about a flute maker? Or a pewter designer or someone who carves pipes out of cattle horns? That's got a bit of flair.

4. What happens when the circus comes to town? Pick a town in your region and get there the night before the circus arrives. If you can't make that story sing, you might think about joining the circus.

5. What's the price of clean water in your region? (This is not a good idea if your region does not have clean water.)

6. Any experiments in wind energy going on in your area? Nobody doesn't like a windmill that is busy generating electricity.

7. And no one dislikes converting animal waste and garbage into usable energy either. Natural elements making energy have a very nice positive ring these days.

8. Has your positive regional published its manual on wood stoves, their use, efficiency, kind of wood to burn, etc.? If it hasn't, it will.

9. What flowers are on the protected list in your region? Don't tell people where to find them—that's what changes endangered into extinct—but you can describe them and say how they came to be protected.

10. How about endangered species? Every region has a bird or animal that is just about the last of its line. Remember the snail darter in Tennessee that held up a multi-million dollar power plant because it was judged endangered by the construction? Find your region's snail darter. Check statistics on declining elk or moose populations in your regional's vicinity. Leave no stone unturned; you might find

a vanishing insect or annelid.

11. Does your region have a return of wild animals? Vermont is seeing its first wolves, coyotes, and moose in many a year. Fox are returning to Virginia.

12. Is there an Indian tribe in your region? There is one in Winooski, Vermont, and I'd be willing to bet you didn't know that if you live outside the state. Go interview a chief or a medicine man. He'll give you a fine story—or hundreds of them.

13. Spend a day at a local heritage festival. What makes the Armenians different from the Italians? Compare foods, songs, customs, etc.

14. Young people are always important in positive publications. Cover a high-school event—a local homecoming week or winter carnival or spring fling. You'll enjoy yourself even if you don't sell the story, but if you let the high schoolers do a lot of talking and if you do a lot of listening, you'll probably sell the story.

15. Is there a group of people in your region who are environmentally isolated—island people, mountain people, prairie or plains people? Is civilization closing in on them? Positive publications would like to hear that it's not.

16. A portrait of a small town always makes good copy. Talk to the librarian, the undertaker, the minister, the town gossip, the storekeeper, the gas pumper. You can't miss if your notes are good and the town wasn't covered by your magazine last year.

17. Is there a real, anything-you-ever-could-hope-for-is-sold-here country store in your region? Even in Vermont, where country stores abound and country store stories are written ever hour or so, I'd still buy a good one for *Vermont Life* if it were to pass my desk.

18. Is there a college or university in your region soon to celebrate its fiftieth year of existence? One hundred years is even better and two hundred years is super. Seventy-five years is so-so.

19. Does your region have weekly band concerts, piano

recitals, outdoor musicals, or jazz festivals? Positive publications are always interested.

20. What's the weather like in your region and who predicts it? Where is the weather station located and how does it run?

21. Do a piece on contrasting styles of home construction. Stories on solar-heated houses have become a cliche, but you could compare modular homes with hand-crafted ones. Or prefabricated buildings with conventionally constructed ones.

22. Or you could give a comparison of architecturally different doorways, windows, fences, roofs, barns, porches. . .this is a list that could get wearisome.

23. How are natural resources mined? I've yet to read an article in defense of strip mining but I'm willing to bet I will before the year is over. Most regionals wouldn't touch a story on how evil nuclear energy is but they might be interested in an intelligent defense of same. And "Ten Ways to Cut Gas Consumption in Nevada" would probably interest the editor of *Nevada*.

24. Take a bicycle tour of your region. What does it look like at that leisurely pace? Or take a hot-air balloon tour or a train tour or a stroll. The editors of positive publications enjoy their readers to be taken by the hand and lovingly presented the territory. Positive publications love to spread the good news. "This place of ours is like no other on earth. Come visit a while."

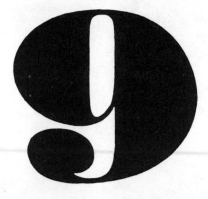

Writing for the Roughnecks

Cashing in on the citymag explosion

City magazines are generally recognized as the most successful regional publications. If you live in a city of any reasonable size, there is a magazine published for you and your fellow residents. If there isn't, there will be soon. City magazines are a fast-growing breed of highly profitable periodicals. They are springing up all over the hemisphere, backed by eager, independent organizations. The city magazine is directed to a specific metropolitan audience and it is intended to serve up more personality, depth, and entertainment than the daily newspapers are able to provide. As the editor of *Westchester* city magazine put it:

> . . .we live in the shadow of the fastest moving, most dynamic city in the world—New York. Our neighbors have their fingers on the pulse of the world each day. We don't want to offer answers to problems, but. . .an understanding of possible alternatives.

Freelancers are in the best possible position to write and sell to city magazines. You're available. You're looking for assignments. Newspapers don't generally allow their staff writers to freelance for area city magazines since competition frequently exists between the two. They are both after the same advertising dollars. The absence of newspaper reporters eliminates a lot of competition. City magazine editors look upon freelancers as a ready source of ideas, with plenty of variety and spark. They know that every writer can offer unique experiences and fresh outlook. City magazines seldom have a single voice. They offer a variety of styles to their readers and just that many opportunities for writers. City magazines are alive and well and loaded with potential.

This wasn't always the case. There was a time, not so long ago, when the only city magazines were those published by local chambers of commerce. They usually sang the praises of their wonderful towns to a dizzying degree and more often than not were supported by donations from local businessmen. A few of these publications still exist but they are not particularly generous to freelancers. The pay is minimal and the benefits are few.

You still have to watch out, too, for small mom-and-pop operations. These types of city magazines usually serve as public relations for relatives, political allies, and friends of the family-run business. Articles rarely feature controversy and are usually fence-sitters where opinions are concerned. They offer little for creative freelancers.

The only time the existence of either a chamber of commerce or mom-and-pop operation really proves helpful to a freelancer is when a new city magazine is moving in on their territory and stirring up competition. Take advantage of the expanding market and establish your own reputation while the new magazine elbows out the old and establishes its name.

The sudden influx of journalistic city magazines was caused by simple advertising economics. In past years— television killed many magazines—including heavyweights like *Life* and *Look*—because it won over the bulk of advertising. But today thirty seconds spent on the air are mighty costly. Half a minute during "Mork and Mindy" on KSTP-TV in St. Paul, Minnesota, costs $1,600. You can understand why advertisers are finding city magazines exciting and economically attractive.

In turn, publishers began finding that city magazines could be lucrative *if* they found the right editorial, advertising, and demographic mix. The *Washingtonian*, a monthly published in D.C., began timidly with eighty pages and a press run of 35,000. At last count, it was 250 pages with 100,000 copies printed. Similar stories could be told about *Philadelphia, San Diego, Chicago*, and *New York*, to name a few. (*San Diego* was the first: it began in 1948. The latest will begin publishing tomorrow.)

The working formula of these successful magazines includes a special tailoring of advertising to demographic mix. You'll find that the advertising is first-rate, fresh, and intriguing. That's because advertising agencies *love* city magazines with their sixty-pound coated stock and above-average color separations. City magazines provide the opportunity for creative people to show their ingenuity. They also furnish advertisers with a sound commercial market.

Who makes up the market? In almost every city magazine, studies show that the readers are affluent, mobile, influential, sophisticated, college-educated, and tend to classify themselves as "elite." It is acknowledged in the publishing industry that city magazines deliver audiences that are higher in income and education (with more of the former, disposable) than practically any other medium.

Louise Damberg, editorial coordinator of *Los Angeles*, sums up her magazine's philosophy this way:

> Our approach to Los Angeles is how to live the best quality of life in the changing, growing, diverse urban-suburban area. . . .The approach is living and doing by upper-income, well-educated residents.

That's why many city magazines are fat with advertising. An advertiser with a brain in his head knows where the action is. It's in the city magazine.

What does that tell you about the contents of those magazines? Plenty. It tells you that stories featuring food-stamp thrift tips and skid row mission menus or articles about muggings and gang fights are not going to interest most city magazine editors. The advertisements will give you potential article ideas if you study them carefully. Numerous ads for figure salons indicate a high awareness of physical appearance, etc.

(When dealing with the more advertising-oriented city magazines, realize that some of them schedule stories up to a year in advance, allowing advertising sponsors to parallel their product with corresponding material. To avoid writing a story that may have already been scheduled, obtain a list of direct mail advertising which the magazine sends to customers. Check for products which may relate to your tentative subject.)

What kind of articles interest city magazine editors? Allen H. Kelson, editor-in-chief of *Chicago*, puts it this way:

> I'm looking for analytical pieces on the persons and activities which result in significant local happenings—not "news" so much as why "news" came to be and the effects of "news" on those involved.
>
> Profiles on significant local figures, celebrated or otherwise.
>
> Service pieces evaluating or commenting on goods, services and establishments which affect readers' lifestyles.
>
> Regular columns covering film, classical music, dance, dining, wine, pop music, local history, books, folk music, art, shopping, etc.

(If one of those departments interests you, and your city magazine doesn't have a regular columnist covering that area, first check back issues to see if your chosen subject was previously featured and then mysteriously disposed of. There may be a reason for its absence. The original author may have written poorly or the local reception to the column story unfavorable. If neither explanation seems to fit the situation and you cannot conceive of any other reasons, don't be bashful about suggesting yourself. Include your list of credentials and sample article copies. No one else is likely to do your promoting for you.)

Special sections on travel, skiing, home electronics. All with as much local orientation as possible.

Studies of lifestyles in particular local areas, or among certain ethnic, cultural, or other social groups whose lifestyles differ from our readers.

Newsy short-takes about often-overlooked or underestimated happenings.

Personal journalism relating to aspects of life in the city.

Specialized one-shot columns on peculiarly local aspects of business, law, personal finance, etc.

Lifestyle pieces dealing with fashions, physical well-being, decorating, personal money management, etc.

Like the editor of every other regional magazine, the editor of *Chicago* is interested in what's happening to his city. Nowhere else. Anything you submit must have local emphasis.

Sometimes it's possible to localize general material and end up with a story suitable for a specific city magazine. You can use a different-than-usual approach and draw a new conclusion. Think in terms of concept. Use your imagination. (This can also be used to spice up an old topic.) A general story on tennis rackets could be localized by visiting area sporting goods stores and comparing prices and selection. Local tennis pros could even be interviewed and share their knowledge on the subject. Be inventive but don't go overboard and come up with forced, obscure local tie-ins. A story highlighting staghorn coral because one of the local aquarium shops stocks it will not sell. Also realize that focusing a story on a local topic isn't sufficient in itself; it must also be well written. And as long as you're being inventive and contriving novel story ideas, don't hestitate to include more than one in the same query letter. (Which should be as well written as your finished story.)

You might try submitting a story on spec. Unlike national markets, city magazines are not generally suffocating with unsolicited manuscripts. In some cases it may produce positive results whereas a query on the same topic may fail. However, this is not a strongly recommended approach.

Since all cities have certain commonalities and many possibilities of general topics, it's possible to employ these similarities and stretch one story idea into two or more. If the story works in Albany, why not give it a shot in Sioux City. Duplicating stories while tailoring to locality is not new. Look at any city magazine and you'll probably find profiles of local disc jockeys, "favorite places for a love affair in St. Louis" (or Memphis or San Francisco), "a jock's guide to San Antonio," "divorce, Toledo-style," "poisonous mushrooms that grow in the city park," "where has all the water gone?" or "where is all the water coming from?" There will be "best" and "worst" lists, hot tips on buying liquor, cigars, wine, trendy clothes, antique automobiles, etc.

Some city magazines are more crusading than others. A quick look at the contents page will separate those that enjoy the heat from those that play it cool. But the editors of *all* city magazines are looking for story ideas.

Now take a quick look at the masthead—under "staff writers." See many? Not likely. City magazines are prosperous but essentially they are also small businesses based on a single concept—the city they promote, denigrate, or assess—and there's little money available for a mob of staff writers. That's where freelancers sidle in. Take a look at that masthead again. Draw conclusions. Who is your competition? (Writers listed as "contributing" are usually preferred.) What writers have speciality columns? Determine the usual number of freelancers. Where do you fit in? There's not a city magazine editor alive who isn't looking for talented writers with fresh ideas.

Many freelancers find that a service article ("how-to,"

shopping comparison, etc.) is a good way to establish yourself initially with a city magazine. The topic is limited, within the city, and comparisons are relatively easy to draw. A short upfront article in a feature section is also a good start. The main thing is to get your foot in the door. Follow through with that first assignment, no matter what, and get credit. Things get easier from there.

As a sometimes inventive freelancer, I've compiled a list that may not work for every city magazine, but the majority of the fifty story ideas that follow should be salable. Each of these ideas can be approached from a number of different directions, and you'll probably want to adjust these ideas in order to make them compatible with the particular city magazine you're writing for.

In the following group of article suggestions you will see frequent references to "your" city. But remember, "your" city can be any metropolitan area you want to write about. Vergennes, Vermont, the third oldest city in New England, has a population of 2,400. New York City's declining population is still over eight million. The thousands of cities that fall in between those two extremes share some things in common with Vergennes and New York. This list is intended to suggest ways in which you might exploit those similarities.

1. Pick a controversy. If your city doesn't have one, you don't have a city. They all have controversies. Shall an underground shopping mall be built? Should the city manager be fired? Should city employees be granted a pay increase? Should firemen be allowed to strike? Pick a controversy and then find a fence-sitter. Every controversy has a fence-sitter but they are the folks whose opinions are never heard. The newspapers devote all their space to the positions of the extremes, despite the fact that people who haven't taken a firm position on a controversy generally make up the majority. Find a good, bright, attractive, articulate fence-sitter, and interview him or her. (You might prep yourself by reading *The Craft of Interviewing* by John

Brady. It is a comprehensive guide to the art of asking questions.)

2. Do a security check. Ask the police, the private detectives and a friendly neighborhood burglar what each thinks might constitute good security for an apartment. (Burglars aren't really that hard to find. Most major cities have associations that help ex-convicts, and most ex-convicts trying to go straight will talk about their days of crime.) Ask all three—the policeman, the detective and the ex-con—what insures protection, what constitutes poor protection and what is regarded as overprotection. Some city people have a tendency to "overisolate" themselves. You could be doing those people a favor by disclosing that multiple bolts, locks, and sounding alarms aren't really necessary. Your research should include a trip to a hardware store to obtain prices of good, solid security equipment. Go to another hardware store and get comparison prices. It's always nice to have a second opinion.

3. Interview two spouses of prominent, local officials, preferably one of each gender (e.g., the wife of the mayor and the husband of the head of the city council). Seat them in a room with a tape recorder and list of questions. How do they feel being married to a public official? How have their lives changed since their partners went public? How do the kids feel about a celebrity parent? How do the spouses feel about playing second fiddle to a celebrity? You can get some mighty good interviews.

4. The first week in November, the American Cancer Society declares "The Great Smoke-Out" and provides lots of publicity in order to encourage people to quit smoking. The local chapter will be more than willing to provide you with all the statistics you can handle on smoking risks, actuarial information, etc. They probably will consent to give you the names of a few folks who pledged to quit last year, during the last "Great American Smoke-Out." Find out if they did, and if not, why not. (For that matter you could interview ex-dieters, former philanderers, or ex-cocaine snorters.) You can report on local organizations which deal with problem smokers and seek out remedy suggestions for "kicking the habit." If you are a smoker, relate personal experiences with quitting, restricted smoking areas, etc.

5. What's coming up at the local museum? A city magazine would certainly be interested in an interview with an artist whose work is currently being displayed. But that means you're going to have to find that artist (sculptor, photographer, weaver, potter, whatever) at least three months before the exhibit to make certain your interview and the magazine's lead times are synchronized. If you have any doubt about the magazine's lead time, just call and ask. If it's the second of January and you call the editorial department of a city magazine and ask what issue they're working on, and they say, "We just put March to bed," or, "We're making assignments for the issue that hits the stands on April twenty-second," then you know what lead time you're dealing with. Ideally you should shoot for six months prior for any story although museums and galleries usually know featured artists at least a year in advance of the exhibits. Time is on your side. You can comfortably budget for query, reply and assignment schedule. Allocating lead time is also important with seasonal story ideas. If a rejection slip is the response to a query, you have enough time to toss the idea to another city magazine before the timeliness of the article is lost.

6. What concerts are scheduled for your area? All the information in the previous paragraph applies here, with one additional suggestion. Don't be overawed by show business personalities. They are almost as human as regional editors but they have something that editors generally lack. Show business people have agents. And agents want their clients to have publicity. Good publicity. An interview in a city magazine during the week of a concert is good publicity, no matter what the interview contains. Scandal sells tickets better than praise, though I'm not proposing that you monger. I'm just suggesting that you go to your city's coliseum, arena, or auditorium and see what the line-up is for the next year or so. Then get your interview. (Telephone interviews are perfectly okay, but if you're taping them, make certain all parties are aware that a machine is recording the words. If you fail to make that known, you're breaking a law.) If your interview turns out to be a good one, and if the interviewee is on a concert tour of sixteen cities, you might just find yourself sitting on sixteen assignments.

7. Follow the building of a new shopping center from initial town-planning board meetings to the ribbon-cutting ceremony. How do the inner-city merchants feel about it? Indignant and unhappy of course, but what action did they take before groundbreaking commenced? Did they attempt to enhance downtown business so that a suburban mall would appear financially unattractive? The new shopping center may be unwelcome competition to inner city merchants but how does the general consumer feel about greater product selection and comparative prices?

8. Find the strangest shop in your city and write about it. But make sure it's really strange. Probably the best you can do in a town like Vergennes, Vermont (population 2,400, remember), is a store that sells seeds and sprouts. But that's Vergennes. Detroit, Providence, and San Diego undoubtedly can do much better. Find yourself an offbeat store and interview the proprietor, the clientele and some folks in the neighborhood. Ask leading questions. Personally sample an unusual food. Single out an exotic product or two. Doesn't your city have a paraphernalia shop?

9. Every city has a restaurant that is family owned and has been for years. The restaurant is ethnic and has superb food at ridiculously low prices. *Every* city has that restaurant and most cities have dozens. Pick one, have a meal there, and write about it. Don't write a review of it—city magazines usually have staff writers rating local cuisine. Write a story. What makes this restaurant special? Does a son or daughter plan to carry on the family tradition? Talk to regular customers and get them to express their loyalty. Describe the place, lovingly.

10. Go behind the scenes of a fashion show, particularly one intended to raise money for charity. Is everything as smooth as silk behind the curtains? Not likely.

11. Apartment decoration articles are always interesting to the readers of city magazines. They like to see how their houses or apartments compare to the ones their city's magazine chooses to spotlight. You might look for decorating ideas that are zany but if you want to write something really original, write a piece on an apartment that is comfortable, pleasant, and ordinary. That's not an easy piece to write. I've never seen it done—but any writer who could put the pieces of that story together would have a gem. City magazine editors, if they have even a vague belief in the Almighty, go to bed praying for gems.

12. Assemble some ex-mayors or retired city officials, as many as you can, in one room. Then get them talking. How do they think the current incumbent is doing? How would they do things differently? What was it like to run their city in the Depression or during the Second World War or during the 1960s? What's the future of this city? (If you know someone who has video equipment, tape this discussion. It could be sold to local television or given to the local historical society.)

13. Does your city have paintings for rent? Most do through local libraries, galleries, or museums. Who rents what and why? Is the Picasso "Blue Period" nude in your boss's executive powder room a recent acquisition? Or did he rent it? How about the art in the homes of the city's moneyed? Rented or bought? Why? The new Matisse in the major hometown firm (e.g. Procter and Gamble, Coca-Cola, Ford, etc.) is it rented? How about the oddest places rented art has ever been, and why?

14. Women executives aren't as rare as they were ten years ago but they aren't as common as they will be ten years from now. An in-depth interview with a woman who manages a store, bank, or manufacturing plant will still make good copy for a city magazine. Before the interview, think of ten questions a newspaper reporter would be most likely to ask a woman executive. (How do you manage your home and your business at the same time? Does femininity help or hinder you on the job? Are you married and is your husband threatened by your career?) Then, make a solemn promise to yourself that you WILL NOT ASK THOSE QUESTIONS. Be original.

15. Speaking of women, who was the first one elected to a high office in your city? An interview with her will be as interesting as your skill allows it to be. If she was elected thirty years ago, don't ask her if she felt she was ahead of her time. Ask her who her favorite movie star was thirty years ago, and if you were around back then, tell her who yours was. Ask her what kind of car she drove and what kind of grades she got in school. Get a conversation going.

16. "How to cope as a single parent" has probably been done by every single major city magazine in North America. But that doesn't mean editors would automatically turn down another good article on that subject if one came along. The number of single parents is on the rise, consequently the interest in the subject has been maintained. But before you do your single-parent-coping story, read one previously printed in your city magazine. Make sure yours has a fresher outlook and more up-to-date information.

17. Is there a new medical procedure in one of your city's hospitals? Doctors will probably be pleased to talk to you about it, *provided* you let it be known from the very beginning that you are entering the discussion with absolutely no knowledge or opinion about the procedure. (If you're in the medical profession yourself, don't let that be known. It will only hurt the interview.) When you understand the medical procedure well enough to explain it to someone ignorant of medical procedures—someone like myself—you've got half your story. The other half will be written for you by patients who have benefited from the new procedure.

18. Attend a city council meeting and find yourself a law being hatched. (It is said in some circles that there are two things the public has no desire to understand the making of: law and sausage. But that's not really true. Law is interesting. It's the sausage we don't want to know about.) Follow the law from its moment of conception to its passage. It might be a good exercise to exclude newspapers as sources of information in this research project. I don't mean to suggest that newspapers will misguide you, but information gathered first hand is always more interesting and is almost always told with more excitement. As you are following this law through meetings and hearings, simultaneously write the story on the assumption that the law will pass. That way, when it does, you can go right to the magazine editor with something very thorough and very timely. If the law doesn't pass. . .well who said freelancing was all fun and roses?

19. Has your city magazine done a story on dog excrement? An editor isn't necessarily looking for a dog excrement story that will outclass his last one, but if that particular subject has been, if you will forgive me, untouched, a first-time-around presentation could be quite amusing. You'd be surprised at how aggravated, exasperated, and defensive people can get on the subject of waste from the alimentary canal of canines. Once this sells, how about a sequel on pigeon droppings?

20. Gardening amidst concrete and tar in high-rises, roof tops, windowsills, or balconies. City people like to grow things, mainly because most cities weren't designated to allow them to. Find out how the local green thumbers are getting the sun shine in and share that information with your city's magazine editor. You are almost sure to find budding interest.

21. A group of couples I know got together one evening and had an auction party. Each couple brought an item or a service which they auctioned off to the other members of the party. One couple auctioned off breakfast in bed, to be served at the time and place of the high bidders' choosing. Another couple auctioned a promise to make an obscene gesture at the public figure of the winners' choice.

Find yourself your own hell-of-a-party and describe it to readers of a city magazine. Better yet, throw one yourself. There are all kinds of parties: tee shirt parties, winetasting parties, parties in which all the attendees arrive with $20 and a suitcase packed for a week in the Bahamas. (At midnight, a name is drawn and that person collects all the money and wins the trip.) Parties can be terrific, and because most people enjoy reading about them, they make good copy. (Of course no intimate details which might outrage the other participants should be revealed.)

22. Man-on-the-street surveys aren't nearly as pedestrian as you might imagine. Every daily newspaper carries some form of man-on-the-street survey in every edition. Sometimes they are hidden in features and other times they are regular columns ("The Inquiring Photographer," etc.). The trick is to think of a good question, and ask that question often enough to make certain that you get nine or ten articulate, off-beat or clever responses. "What did you do on your last vacation?" is not a good question, nor is "What would you do with $1 million?". On the other hand, "What do you think aout ears?" is. How about "Why can't people tickle themselves?" or "What is the very last thing you do before you get into bed at night?"

23. Take ten prominent people in your city and find out where they go when they want to get away from it all. Do they have a special room where they can have mini-nervous breakdowns in private? Do they own an island or a hunting lodge? Where do these prominent people go when they want to be alone? (Relate only general concepts, not specific locations. They'll be forever grateful.)

24. The same question posed to unprominent but interesting people is just as good a story. Where does a priest go when he's had it up to his collar with confessions? Where does a nurse in a cancer ward go when she doesn't want to let people see her cry? Where does the butcher go? (He knows how to make sausage.) Or the owner of the local drycleaning store? Most important in this piece is you. Air your own idiosyncrasies. Where do you go when city life seems to be closing in too fast?

25. How about an interview with people who hate jogging and joggers, or biking and bikers, or roller skating and skaters? Or you could set up a round-table discussion with those that do and those that don't. Watch the sparks fly and make sure your tape recorder doesn't run out of tape. They have a habit of doing that just when the good stuff gets started.

26. I live in Montpelier, Vermont, am reasonably well-known by my fellow Montpelierites and because I am the editor of the state magazine, enjoy a degree of status. People think they know me. But how many people know I spend approximately one hour a day throwing darts?

Why not write an article on executive hobbies? Go for good hobbies like mine. Forget about the golfers, tennis players, stamp collectors, and antique freaks. Go for the closet dart throwers. We make better copy.

27. Visit a city pet store. Spend a day there. If you don't bring a tender, heartrending (or cynical) story home to your typewriter that evening, you're not cut out for this business.

28. Every city has people who work in it and live outside it. They commute. Find out what that's all about in your city and write about it. Who commutes? Why do they? Who comes the farthest? By what transportation means? (A group of men who live on Long Island, New York, commute four hours each direction to a shipyard in Philadelphia, Pennsylvania. Want to know why? The answer is written on their paychecks.) Do some commuting yourself. What's your verdict? Are people car-pooling? Do they travel the same way every day or look for new routes? If they found a job next door that paid precisely the same as the job they are commuting to, would they take it? I'm told that some people enjoy commuting. You might find out why on earth they do.

29. City magazines love to do what daily newspapers can not. Let me give you a local example. In Burlington, Vermont, a middle-aged, middle-class woman drove her teenage daughter to a parking lot one Saturday afternoon, asked her to step out of the car, and shot her five times with a pistol. She then immediately turned herself over to police authorities, eventually pleaded guilty to second-degree murder, and is currently residing in a correctional institution.

The newspapers reported that the woman believed her daughter was planning to move to Boston and become a prostitute. Rather than let her do that, she wished her daughter dead and accomplished that grisly ultimate in child abuse with a handgun. That's what the newspapers had to offer.

But was there more to it? Of course there was, but the newspapers had neither the space nor the manpower to uncover the whole story. They couldn't send a reporter to Boston to find out if the girl really was going to enter the oldest profession. They couldn't talk to the judge who sentenced the mother, or talk to the father to find out how he felt, or talk to the girl's friends and classmates. Newspapers can't offer that kind of in-depth research.

City magazines can. Find an interesting news story, and then get the real story. All you have to do first is read your city newspaper.

30. Every city has at least one couple (and most have countless) who live together without the benefit of a marriage license or official ceremony, and who are absolutely itching to tell the world about it. Let them. Just make certain your article doesn't make a moral judgment or lets your own personal bias show through. Let it just be their microphone. (If the couple shares not only one apartment but one gender, check your city magazine's editorial policy.)

31. Almost every city but Vergennes, Vermont (which doesn't have a city magazine anyway), has the potential for a get-away-from-it-all weekend within its limits. It could be a splendidly posh hotel, a nunnery, or a hermit's cave. Find it, get away from it all for a weekend, and write about it.

32. City magazines have audiences who would rather not grow old. (So do religious, machine tool, and veterinary magazines, but their readers are not of interest at the moment.) The quest for eternal, or at least lingering, youth involves face-lifts, hair transplants and implants, magic creams and jolly jellies. Go to a few retail outlets that specialize in these wonder products and talk to their patrons and owners. Be careful not to be condescending. You'll be talking to some pretty serious people.

33. I am willing to wager that your city has a woman living in it who is alone but not lonely, poor but not impoverished, old but not infirmed, proud but not defiant. You can find her by asking people at a church or synagogue where she lives. At first, when you go to her home and say you want to write a story about her, she'll be sincerely diffident. "Who on earth would want to read a story about me?" she'll ask. "*I* would," you might respond, "but instead, I'd like to write it." (Actually, that's not going to be quite true. She'll write the story. All you'll do is jot the words down.)

34. An elderly gentleman. The same as above.

35. Does your city have a professional sports team of any kind? Is there any sport you know absolutely nothing about? If I were the editor of a magazine in Dallas, Texas, and you wrote me a query telling me that you had never seen a football game in your entire life and you don't know a touchdown from a rubdown but you'd like to do a piece in the Dallas Cowboys' locker room after a home game, and if you assured me that you had reasonable writing credentials, I'd give you the assignment. It would be difficult to make that story *anything* but hilarious.

36. Write an article about jobs that people must not take home with them. Welfare workers, criminal court judges, surgeons, maybe even oil company executives. Every city has its own segment of the working population which must, for reasons having mostly to do with sanity, leave their jobs behind them when they go home in the evening. Talk to them. And *listen* to them.

37. Know anyone waiting to adopt a baby? Ask around and you'll probably find numerous couples in any city waiting for that special phone call. Get to know several and let them understand what you have in mind, and then ask permission to be with them from the moment that phone call comes until the end of that day. That's the kind of story that practically writes itself, provided you are not part of it. It is definitely not a first person story. The author should be thoroughly invisible.

38. Sons and daughters of celebrities like nothing less than publicity based on their lineage. But since they've been on the rim of the limelight ever since their parent or parents became famous for whatever reason, they will probably know how to deal with writers. That means they're probably not going to want to talk to you and give you a usable interview. That is, unless you convince them that they are interesting subjects in their own right. This may take a superlative degree of smooth talking, but try touching upon personal interests, hobbies, activities until you get a conversation going. And because city magazines are celebrity conscious, the editor is going to be interested in that conversation.

39. Every writer who has ever thought of writing for a city magazine has thought that the city's oldest living citizen is a perfectly natural story. Usually, the idea goes no further than that. Some writers do go as far as finding out who the city's oldest citizen is (Social Security records or city clerk offices can provide that information) but when the writer finds out that Mr. Pierce, who was born 103 years ago, lives in the Shady Rill Rest Home, he is often reluctant to pursue the story any further. Some writers don't think any first class story could originate in a nursing home. I suggest that you take it from there. Go to the Shady Rill Rest Home and find

Mr. Pierce. Congratulate him and then ask him what mixed drinks he avoids.

40. Interview the editor of the city magazine for which you are hoping to write. It is unlikely that he or she will turn you down—at least not for the interview. And if the editor ultimately tells you that he couldn't possibly publish your article, that it would appear far too self-serving, ask if he has any suggestions about where such an article might be published. Then be prepared to get a whole lot of helpful information.

41. A teacher I know at a city school had a dandy idea about how to teach his sixth graders a bit about money, arithmetic, social studies, and life. He gathered up a few old Monopoly sets and distributed $500 in play money to each of his seventeen eager, wide-eyed students. He then told them they could spend the money among themselves any way they wanted; they could buy homework assignments from each other, buy lunches, sell chores or old baseball gloves—use it any way they saw fit. At the end of a month, the teacher explained, the class would see how much money each student had and what the experience had taught him or her.

At the end of the month, one little girl had over $4,000 in play money, one boy had just less than $2,000, and the rest of the pupils in the class were in varying stages of debt, loss and gain.

Find yourself an interested teacher and write about one of his or her projects. City magazine editors occasionally enjoy making their readers smile.

42. Why are diet books always best sellers? I can't give you the answer to that question: weight has never been one of my problems. But the way diet books sell tells me that I'm not in the majority. As I said earlier, the city magazine is aimed at people who are likely to be upwardly mobile, affluent, well-educated, and slender. Or trying to be slender. Why not give them a diet?

If you choose to look on the lighter side, you might just make one up. But you'd better make it for lunches only, just to be certain that no one goes to their Greater Reward because they followed your advice three meals a day for thirty days. Call it "The St. Paul Minneapolis Executive Lunch Diet." It could be watercress on rye with a bottle of Saratoga Springs water and an olive. But make it absolutely clear that the diet is an exaggerated spoof.

If you decide to write with a more serious tone it will take a little more work. You'll have to confer with a registered dietition or a nutrition specialist so you can present a regimen which is generally regarded as safe and nutritionally sound. Still caution would-be dieters to consult a physician before starting. (And who knows, you may shed some extra poundage yourself.)

43. Live life with a home computer for a week and then write about it. Home computers are not terribly expensive to rent or program. If you told a computer manufacturer that you were writing a story on the experience of using his product in your home, he most likely would be delighted with the publicity and lend you the computer free of charge. (Remember, it's not improper to say "I am writing an article for *New York* magazine and I was wondering if you would. . . ." It *is* improper, and a bad idea, to say "I have been assigned to do an article for *New York* magazine. . ." if that assignment was never actually made. That's why I suggest that you always query first. And if the editor indicates that he is willing to look at what you produce, with no promises, you can legally and morally and honestly say "I am writing a magazine article."

44. Is there a dress designer in your city? There is in Vergennes, Vermont. I suggest you find one in yours and then follow a dress from the day it was conceived to the day it was presented to the public in a fashion show. Who bought it? Who's wearing it today?

45. Almost all public television stations hold auctions annually to raise operating capital. The problem with writing about them for your city's magazine is always lead time; by the time you've watched the auction and recorded all the zany and humorous and heartwarming stories that are sure to be happening behind the scenes, the magazine you want to write for will be in the midst of planning an issue three or four months down the road. The trick to the auction story is to get behind the scenes before the televised action begins. Get to the chairman of fund raising and learn some advance information. What sort of items are being auctioned off? Who are some of the guest auctioneers going to be? Did anything happen at last year's auction that was particularly amusing, dreadful, surprising or joyous? How much money was made last year? What is the station shooting for this year?

That story can be written well in advance and published while the event is actually going on. City magazines *love* to be timely like that.

46. Auctions that don't demand timeliness are one-time affairs—businesses that have gone under, estates that are being settled, or even municipal institutions which are updating their equipment and unloading everything they no longer need. There is always a story at an auction. I once wrote one for the *New York Times* on a very sad auction. The owner of a small household estate was present at the auction and as she watched the accumulation of her lifetime sold off at ridiculously low prices to strangers, she wept. Other auctions lean in the opposite direction. I've read in the *New York Daily News* about an amusing auction in which the folks that run the U.S. Customs Service at the Port of New York were auctioning off items that had gone unclaimed for five or more years. Lots of suitcases, of course (that had been cleared of contraband by authorities—again, of course) but lots of bizzarre items as well. One high bidder won a railroad car filled with hair dryers. Another took home a huge plastic bag full of left shoes without mates.

Go cover an auction. There's got to be a story in it.

47. Every city has a historic landmark that is going to be restored because the federal government has funneled a huge amount of money to keep that city looking like it used to. The problem is to get that story to the editor of your city's magazine before anyone else does. By the time the money is officially handed over, newspapers will have covered the event thoroughly and when your magazine editor reads your "story of the restoration" proposal, a glazed look will come over his face.

The solution is to go to your state historic preservation division and find out if its operators have their eyes on any vulnerable buildings in the city of your choice. "Yes," they might say. "Those idiots down at city hall are talking about tearing down the old public bathhouse." "Oh," you say. "Thank you very much. I'm afraid I have to run now. I have a query to write."

48. What is the most exclusive club in your city? What country club or men's or women's club is positively the most snobby, snooty, uppity club in town? A readable first-person article might be put together if you tried to join that club, and then listed all the reasons your potential membership was out of the question. You might also tell readers who is a member of the club. City magazine readers love to know who the insiders are.

49. Spend a day at a firehouse, and if a fire occurs that day, plan to come back another time. The idea is to do a story on a typical day at the firehouse—a day on which there are no alarms. (Needless to say, the bigger the city, the fewer typical days there will be. But if you're writing this article for a big city magazine, pick a fire station in a nice, quiet, arsonist-free neighborhood.) How do firemen spend the day when they're not putting out fires? Is all that maintenance really necessary or is it just a lot of busy work? (But, don't fire that rude question.) When a little boy says he wants to be a fireman when he grows up, should he be told he's in for a life of brief excitement spanned by boredom?

50. Does your city have a Rotary Club, Civitan Club, Lions Club, and Kiwanis Club? Their members are almost always allowed, and even encouraged, to bring guests. Make use of your connections and have friends invite you to a meeting of each one. Then write about your civic experiences. Don't pick close friends because you're probably not going to keep them after your article appears. Not if you write it as hilariously as you should.

There are fifty ideas that with a little help from you could be multiplied numerous times. City magazines are looking for new approaches to urban realities. Don't be afraid to innovate.

When you've got an assignment from a city magazine remember (as in *all* freelance writing) that everything counts. The common complaint by city magazine editors is that many freelancers lack professionalism: they're not dependable; they don't realize the importance of a deadline. So if you assume a deadline—meet it. Honor length requirements. Thoroughly research your facts. If you play your cards right, a city magazine can give you the exposure you need to establish your name as a writer of note.

10

Ever On Sunday

Newspapers' weekly regionals

They aren't quite magazines and they aren't quite newspapers. Some have circulations in the millions, others in the thousands. A few pay top dollar for freelance material, a few pay almost nothing. The ones in between pay decently and are looking for writers with regional ideas. They happen every Sunday and they are called "newspaper inserts."

The *Los Angeles Times*, the *New York Times*, *Chicago Tribune*, *Detroit Free Press*, *St. Louis Post-Dispatch*, *Washington Star*, and other newspapers of their clout and size have inserts that would correctly be called magazines. The *New York Times Sunday Magazine* often runs over one hundred pages and is filled with service columns, news features on topical events of national significance, profiles of prominent New York-connected personalities (which would include Sen. Bill Bradley of New Jersey, who used to play foreward for the New York Knicks basketball team, and Henry Kissinger of Manhattan who used to play whatever for the Nixon Administration). The *Times* magazine is a weekly necessity of millions of East Coast residents and I know a lot of adults who seem to suffer more than simple cultural deprivation when they have to get through an entire Day of Rest without theirs. I know other people who write for the *Times* magazine, and I know their paychecks have been in four figures.

I was once assigned to write a piece about Christmas tree harvesting by the *Times* magazine senior editor, giving it the New York slant by following a tree from its roots in Vermont to its decoration in a Fifth Avenue apartment. I wrote the piece and handed it in on time. Several days later the senior editor called me. She sounded not so good.

"We had a meeting with the editorial board and they don't like your story. I feel just awful because I *love* the story. But they just didn't think it was right fot the *Times*. Would you possibly accept a $200 kill fee?"

I said I certainly would, had the piece returned to me, did some cosmetic changes (Fifth Avenue became Quincy Avenue) and sold it to the *Boston Globe* Sunday magazine for $300. I had paid a research assistant $100 to find out everything she could about Christmas trees so I netted $400 for about four hours' work.

I tell the above story not to bask in my own glory but to make two points. First, when you are *assigned* to write something, and it doesn't work out somehow, you are owed some money. One-fifth of what you might have normally received is about the average kill fee. The second point has to do with resale. After the *Times* rejected my story, it immediately became my property again. I could do anything with it I wanted to, and what I wanted to do was find a new market. Boston seemed a logical choice because I happened to know that as many Vermont Christmas pines and spruces ended up in Boston as New York. Since the story essentially took place in Vermont, I felt no ethical misgivings about switching the ultimate destination of my little tree.

When I tell the story of the *Times* rejection-*Globe*

acceptance on social occasions, I get two opposite reactions about my use of a researcher. Some people are outraged that I gave someone one-fifth of my total earnings when she did twice as much work as I did. Other people say I am exploiting high-school seniors by making them do practically all my work for me.

When I point out that the high-school student was getting paid more than $10 an hour for work that was informative, interesting, and ideal training for a career in writing, I get a different kind of reaction. They become outraged that I didn't ask their son or daughter to do my legwork.

It's a paradox I've learned to live with. I don't really enjoy researching. It's getting behind a typewriter that gets my juices flowing. I make certain that the person I get to do my research is dependable, enthusiastic, and not likely to be distracted. If I say I need notes by Friday, that's because I'm on a deadline and plan to have the piece in the mail no later than Sunday afternoon. If a researcher calls me on Thursday and says she broke up with her boyfriend and can't possibly concentrate on the assignment, I permanently remove her name from my list of researchers. I also make a mental note to have words with whoever it was who recommended her, because that person has put me in a bind. I have to do my own research now, and in a hurry. And I have a full-time job that is occasionally even more than full-time. That little lovesick lady put me in a bad mood.

If you enjoy researching articles, newspaper inserts and magazines are the ideal regional publication for you. The very essence of their editorial make-up is articles which need thorough investigation, probing and searching and scrutinizing. Newspaper inserts and magazines do for their regions what the newspapers that are wrapped around them every Sunday can not do. With very few exceptions, newspapers today find investigative journalism or long, in-depth features a luxury they can't afford. (The Wall Street Journal is an exception. They can afford to send reporters on investigations for up to a year, but that's a special case. The

WSJ not only doesn't have a Sunday insert, it doesn't have a Sunday edition.) The inserts, on the other hand, *can* be leisurely, or even long-winded. The people who write for them don't have to meet daily deadlines; the pressures of immediacy and timeliness diminish in Sunday supplements. As a result, the writing in most of them is better. The writers have had breathing room. Their editors have had a chance to wield a heavy pencil, or even time to send it back to the writer with suggestions on how to hone the piece or breathe more life into it.

But what sort of material are the editors of Sunday inserts looking for? The most direct way to get an answer to that is to ask directly. Writer's guidelines are often available upon request. "Articles must be timely and reflect trends," says the editor of the *New York Times Sunday Magazine*. "We're always looking for writers who have never published before. We're *not* looking for political columnists." Full-length articles for this publication run from 2,500 to 5,000 words and pay $850 and up.

Today magazine, the Sunday supplement to the *Philadelphia Inquirer*, has a circulation of less than 200,000 and pays between $250 and $500 for articles of up to 5,000 words.

The *Rhode Islander* out of Providence has a circulation of 210,000, pays between $50 and $200 and, according to its editor, "Is always on the lookout for new writers with real talent."

Parade, which has made America its region and is distributed to newspapers as a Sunday supplement, has a circulation of over 19 million. "We're interested in features that will inform, educate or entertain a mass circulation, domestic audience," says the editor. "A good way to start with us is if you have particular experience in some field. Another advantage to the new writer would be competence with a camera."

Empire magazine out of Colorado covers six states and pays five cents a word with 2,500 words maximum. The *Indianapolis Star* magazine pays between $25 and $75 per article, while the *Billings Gazette* out of Montana pays 25 cents per column inch. Circulations and payments vary greatly. So do format and style and lead time. (The *Time* magazine might claim to want "timeliness" but they have decided most of the contents of their weekly offering six weeks in advance. Smaller, more localized Sunday supplements will need to know at least by Tuesday what they will print Saturday night.)

But all supplements have these things in common:

—They are generally intended for local audiences, not tourists. "Local" could mean the town of Gatlinburg, Tennessee, or the Province of Montreal, but the readership has been tagged as permanent, not transient.

—Sunday supplements are seldom interested in history, unless it has a modern twist. There is even less interest in fiction.

—The newspaper inserts and magazines are interested in articles that can expand upon information that previously appeared in the newspaper that carries them.

Six Basic Article Formats

The Expanded Who, What, When, and Where Article appears in every newspaper at least a dozen times—and that's on a slow news day. The form is classic Journalism: get the who, what, where, and when tucked into the lead paragraph. The rest of the information follows in order of its importance. This "pyramid style" writing allows a newspaper editor to cut the piece at any point and know that he is losing the less important information.

I once wrote a "Who, What, Where, When" lead for a newspaper I worked for that came close to being a very good lead.

A Bristol, Tennessee man walked into a State Street restaurant at noon today, took a hook-blade knife from his jacket pocket and walked over to a corner booth where he savagely slashed his wife to death.

That has all the essential information. The lead only made

one mistake: it lacks the word "allegedly." (Years later, when a newspaper editor was reviewing my portfolio and, after reading that lead, asked incredulously how I could possibly omit the traditional qualifier, I explained that I was eating lunch at the restaurant at the time of the "alleged" incident and had helped subdue the man moments after the tragic event. "That," the editor told me, "is a poor excuse.")

A story for a Sunday supplement about the alleged murderer, his motives and capture and subsequent trial, could also contain who, what, where and when information. It could be written as a traditional news story in the pyramid style. But it would have the advantage of a greater perspective and the developments that gave the story more depth.

An article that appeared in a daily newspaper about a trend in Bordentown, New Jersey, began like this:

> Voters in this community of 5,000 have told their city leaders that they want welfare recipients—when able—to be put to work. Dubbed "Workfare," the new plan has caused the number of people applying for welfare to fall off 90 percent within the last four months.

When the story of Bordentown appeared in *Parade* magazine, the lead went like this:

> Chiseled in a granite tombstone erected in front of City Hall in Bordentown, N.J. are the words: In memory of the New Jersey welfare bureaucracy.

A much more regional approach in the Sunday supplement. Yet the original news story and the relaxed feature both follow the same format. The important information was near the beginning of both pieces and as the story progressed, the facts assumed less prominence.

The Interpretive or Investigative Article is another regular feature of Sunday supplements. They, too, are often deadline. The writer or reporter chooses his own deadline and picks that moment to bring the investigation to a close or the interpretation to a conclusion.

The major difference between it and an article written in the pyramid style is that an Investigative or Interpretive article could save the best for last. A writer for *Dayton Leisure*, a weekly Ohio supplement, may write 2,900 words on the subject of skateboards and then conclude with 100 words saying he thinks they should be banned. That could be effectively accomplished. A writer for *Northeast* magazine could wonder aloud for quite a while whether Oregon was first settled by roaming Russian fishermen—cite facts that both supported and refuted such a notion—and then offer his own theory.

The Article of Opinion is found in nearly every Sunday supplement. It may take the form of Russell Baker's consistently mirthful essays in the *Times* magazine or offer advice, as does the column "Ask Beth" in the Boston *Globe*'s *New England* magazine. ("Beth" is Elizabeth Winship, wife of *Globe* editor Thomas Winship, and she also gives very sound advice.) An article of opinion could be a movie review or a first-person complaint about the proliferation of malls. It can be anything that expresses a personal view, on any subject the Sunday supplement is interested in promoting or presenting.

The How-To Article makes editors of newspaper inserts and magazines smile, when written with style as well as clarity. "How to Insulate Your Apartment This Summer and Save Half Your Electricty Bill Next Winter" would probably be read eagerly by any supplement editor. The key in a "how-to" is to make things simple. Remember, the readership includes everyone who reads the daily newspaper and that includes all us plain folks. If you want to tell me how to insulate my house this summer, you almost have to start by explaining what a ladder is.

The Round-Up or Summary Article gathers information from many sources and it secures them under a single by-line. "The Ten Safest Mines in West Virginia" would do nicely in the *Sunday Gazette Mail of East Charleston*. *Vermonter*, published every Sunday by the *Burlington Free*

Press, wouldn't mind seeing a piece on "Burlington's All Time Hockey All-Star Team" or "Sixteen Vermont Inns Waiting to be Discovered." The *Washington Post* magazine has had it up to there with senatorial sex lives and the high cost of living in D.C. but try "A Dozen Summer Vacation Spots, A Half Tank Away" and see what kind of interest you generate.

The Profile Article is the last staple of the Sunday supplement. Pick a personality whose lifestyle or accomplishments or star staus would make him or her interesting to your potential readers. You can write a profile in the first person nicely:

> When I arrived at actress Susan Dey's Los Angeles apartment recently, I was surprised to see her carrying an infant girl.
> "Susan, I didn't know," I said.
> "Sarah," she replied, and looked admiring at her first-born.
> "Quite a production," I said and she ushered me into the house she shares with producer-husband, Leonard Hirsham.

Your profile doesn't have to be a celebrity, or even semi-so. A good, strong interview with the regular bartender at a popular downtown nightspot ought to move any insert editor. One of the best profiles I've read in these part was written about a woman who does various voices in local radio commericals. She also was a waitress, one I tipped on a regular basis in my home town.

Those six formats cover every story possibility for newspaper inserts—even ones that come out on Saturday.

Sunday supplements are also almost exclusively written by freelancers (of all regional publications the supplements have the highest freqency). They represent a weekly windfall for people with fresh ideas, time to develop them, and the need for an occasional by-line and check in order to insure emotional stability.

Sunday supplements and newspaper inserts are a potential goldmine for writers who know a good story when they see one. Sometimes the regional insert is the *last* place a writer thinks about trying to peddle his wares. The slicker magazines pay more, and they offer a more lasting and more prestigious platform. But the inserts' frequency makes them valuable to writers who are looking for regional outlets. Insert editors are looking for writers they can count on, and if there's a difference between $25 a week and $300 a quarter, it's the difference between one by-line and a dozen.

11

How Green is Your Pasture?

Writing for environmental regionals

Identifying an environmental regional magazine is a logical first step toward writing for one. Just what constitutes this breed?

First, there are no terribly firm lines. Some magazines seem to be environmentally conscious—certainly the positive publications are—without taking specific and hardnosed stands. Practicality often forbids topicality. The beautiful magazines often need six months or more to get dressed; the issue they might like to take a stand on could be resolved while they're going to press. But environmental regionals do take stands. They have specific points of view, reflections of their publishers' biases, and they present them in their pages.

Who are the publishers? *Wonderful West Virginia* is published by that state's Department of Natural Resources, and it carries articles titled "The Importance of the State Park System," "Hunting and Fishing Licenses are a 'Heck of a Bargain,' " and "Calendar of Nature Events." *North Dakota*

Horizons is published by the Greter North Dakota Association and features articles like "Gumbo Gardening in the Red
River Valley" and "Wildflowers of North Dakota." *Outdoors
in Georgia* was published by the Georgia Board of Natural
Resources. When the legislature reduced that board's
budget, the magazine was the first to go. (Subscribers were
completely reimbursed for unfulfilled subscriptions, but the
magazine's staff had a less generous fate.) The *New York
Conservationist* is published by that state's Conservation
Society. One look at the contents page and the masthead will
tell you a lot about any environmental regional. If the
magazine is funded by a government source, it's likely to
contain more puffery about the region than if the money
comes from a private organization.

The money comes from *somewhere*, and it's important to
find out where if you are going to write for an environmental
regional. The money, in almost every case, does *not* come
from subscriptions or advertising. There's usually a sugar
daddy back there somewhere, and finding out what he, she,
or it is will be very helpful as you're putting together a story
idea.

If the sugar daddy is governmental and official, forget
about any antinuclear power stories. Don't bother protesting
the building of a major hydroelectric dam, and discard the
notion that you are going to break the mold and get a piece
published on the evils of suburban growth. You're not. The
editors aren't going to be interested. They're being supported
and are not about to bite the hand that supports them. That is
not to suggest that their magazines spinelessly tremble
under a bureaucratic gaze. It just means that the function
government has set for them is environmentally optimistic.
Easy on the negatives.

Privately owned magazines with an environmental slant
can get a little more controversial. Their editors can muddy
up the waters a bit. "Since the Adirondack Park is the scene
of a major experiment in land-use planning for conservation
purposes, we find it impossible to avoid controversy

altogether," says *Adirondack Life* editor Bernard R. Carmen. "We bill ourselves as the 'magazine of life in the East's last wilderness,' and much of our content is dedicated to supporting that proposition."

Carmen's counterpart on the other side of the Great Divide is Mark O. Thompson, editor of privately owned *Montana* magazine. "This is one of the last remaining places in the country where the pace of life is not dehumanizingly rushed," he says. "Montana's scale is vast beyond the imagination of most people, yet it is threatened by its very beauty and appeal to city emigrants. Montana is also threatened by a demand for her natural resources. The magazine's purpose is to reflect that beauty and that sense of scale, but with a conservation ethic."

Other magazines that could be called "environmental" (because they show a lot of their regions' outdoors and speak in terms of conservation and environmental restraint) shy away from outright contest. "We don't publish much social commentary or controversy," says Jill Weber Dean, managing editor of the privately owned quarterly, *Wisconsin Trails*. "But we are willing to consider it."

Wisconsin Trails may publish a piece on "Town Meeting in Honey Creek in Sauk County," and the biggest question before the voters might, indeed, be the pollution of a nearby stream by a soon-to-be constructed lumber processing plant. But the piece that runs in the magazine will deal much more with democracy in action and the homey informality of that annual ritual. When the magazine does run a story about an industrial plant, it will pick something benign, like the Kohler Company in Sheboygan County (the world's foremost manufacturer of bathtubs).

When you find a regional environmental and have figured out who is doing the talking (public or private) and what the tone of voice is (strident or tranquil), you're in a pretty good position to assess the audience. If the magazine is published by the Department of Parks and features articles on Ranger Chuck, family campgrounds, and milkweed pod collecting, you can be pretty sure its readers are soft on motor homes and dirt bikes. If the magazine, on the other hand, protests all-terrain vehicles and plastic packaging, you are probably safe in guessing the readership is largely young, restless, and not Republican.

Now you're ready to write. You know whom you are talking to and by whose authority.

The question is, are you still interested? Environmental regionals need you, but as a writer, do you need them?

Maybe not. Certainly the pay from environmental regionals runs well below any other group of regionals. The privately owned magazines pay in direct proportion to how successful they are. *Bend of the River* magazine of Perrysburg, Ohio, pays $5 for articles and $1 for photographs. *Coast* magazine of Myrtle Beach, South Carolina, pays between $10 and $35 for articles. *Bluenose* magazine of Port Maitland, Nova Scotia, pays one cent a word, *Outdoor Indiana* pays two cents a word. *Missouri Life* pays up to $100 for feature-length pieces, and *Montana* pays up to $300. *British Columbia Outdoors* starts writers at 7½ cents a word and *Incredible Idaho* finishes some writers off with this note on its writers' fact sheet: "No payment is being made for articles at this time, but multiple complimentary copies are mailed to contributors."

The rates are on the low side but the research required can and often does run in the opposite direction. If you're doing a piece that deals with timber and reforestation of a particular newly designated natural area, you can't gather research from your overstuffed recliner. If you're writing on the effects of pesticides in destroying food for birds, you're going to have to face up to the fact that you'll be inspecting a dead duck or two. If your piece discusses the vandalism of an area's natural landmarks, you might even have to put yourself in some rough company. You could get hurt.

And for multiple complimentary copies?

Not likely.

But there is another side to writing for environmental

regionals, a side that makes them downright appealing.

It depends on the nature of the magazine, of course, but the environmental publications usually offer subject areas that you can sink your editorial teeth into.

In the environmental publications, you can write about what you really love. You can show off your expertise with pride and you can imply that your readers are missing something essential if they can't share what you are offering.

But in environmental magazines, the material is authentic and the readers do want to share. You are writing for a sophisticated audience; readers who want to know what you have to say, but expect your delivery to be precise, scientific, reliable. Don't try to fool Mother Nature's readers.

Even the most stuffy, official agency-run quarterly is interested in well-written pieces on canoeing, kayaking, fishing, camping, backpacking, alpine-slide sliding, boating, bird watching, and where applicable, snowshoeing, skiing, snowmobiling, and ice skating.

Less stuffy publications are interested in even more: the growing popularity of hydro-power, the destruction of tender vegetation on trails, efforts to preserve natural beauty without eliminating public use, weather and its effect on the environment, profiles of people who pioneered in the development of wilderness areas—these would all interest editors of most middle-of-the-road environmental publications.

And then, of course, you have what I call the "antees." (Oops. Am I about to reveal a rent in my otherwise intact and universal love for humankind?) The antees are the environmental publications that are against a whole lot of things. They are antinuclear and antihunting and antitrapping and antimechanization, and the radical members of this breed are antifishing, anti-anything that has smoke coming out of it, anti-having any more babies (except when delivered by a midwife, at home, with most of the neighborhood in attendance), anti-everything that starts only when it's plugged in, and anti-anything else that might advance civilization past about the sixth century, A.D. Except for stereos with headphones. And Mateus Rosé bottles.

But those publications don't pay very much and, because their readers eventually stumble (often unwittingly) into maturity, they don't last very long. Many antees are short-lived and cheap. But interesting. And even when they are at their negative worst, when they have hit new heights of nihilism, they still present their writers with a platform.

Some antees, of course, do survive and even, perhaps, prevail. The Clamshell Alliance, with many responsible members and a particularly singular purpose, has newsletters all over the country that preach to the already-converted about the evils of atomic energy. So do Friends of the Earth. This type of publication depends largely on volunteer efforts, but they do provide platforms for new writers. I would only offer this word of caution. Don't believe that by writing an impassioned "save-the-whale" article you will influence one single whale hunter in any significant way. Because you won't. Whale hunters read the *Whale Hunter Quarterly* or *Bering Straits Bulletin* and maybe *Field & Stream*.

Other people read magazines like *Rod and Gun*, *Backpacker*, the *Maine Sportsman*, and *Fly Fishermen*. In fact, if whale hunters represent one end of an extreme and whale-savers represent the other, most of us who are left are somewhere in-between. Leaning, maybe, but in-between.

For us, there are hundreds of environmental magazines to read, to write for, to illustrate. Virtually every region has a sports publication dedicated to the hunters and fishermen in its area. This marvelously well-defined audience is also sophisticated about its view of the environment. You'll never sell a story to the *Vermont Sportsman* on the evils of shooting a white-tailed deer with a high-powered rifle, but you might be able to peddle a piece on where the most expensive hunting rifle is made and who makes it. Similarly, a story on possible pollution problems on the shores of Lake Huron would go very nicely in the *Angler and Hunter in Ontario*. If you spent a week in the Brooks Range observing Dall sheep, *Alaska Bowman* might be interested. Catch a three-pound "rainbow" in the Blue River? Pete Heley of the *Oregon Angler* would love to know about it and will pay $30 or more for the privilege.

You might send along a photograph of that trout. And that advice goes for almost every other environmental publication. Don't talk about your subject. *Show* it. Only the most sophisticated environmenal magazines—*Audubon*, *American Forests*, and the *Sierra Club News*, for example—have photography staffs of their own. Most of the others are looking for freelance illustration to go along with freelance writing.

Some environmental publications are looking for dirty pictures. Scenes showing smoke billowing out of a factory at sunset, or bumper-to-bumper traffic on the Los Angeles freeway, or a porpoise washed up on Miami Beach. Some of these publications like to make their point by explicitly showing what can happen when we ignore the environment. It's a good idea to see what the photographic policy of the publication is before submitting anything at all.

To be successful writing for any environmental regional, you have to care. If that reads like a vast generalization and over-simplification, it is not. You don't have to care to write about how to bake a strawberry cheesecake or about quarrying for granite. You don't have to care about basketball to write convincingly and well about a high-school senior who stands seven foot two and can dribble like a magician. You don't have to care about the museums of Dayton, Ohio, in order to write about those places. A couple of visits and some free brochures is all you'll need.

But to write about the environment, you have to really care about the environment. Unfortunately, most environmental writers care so much, they've forgotten how to smile. "What's funny about a melt-down at a thermonuclear plant?" they might say to me, and I'm not sure what I'd say back. I don't know the lighter side of nuclear fission; I stayed clear of that in college.

But I do know editing and editors. And most of them, like me, are looking for writers with a sense of history and humor and heart. We are looking for writers who have perspective, who know that we humans can be terribly silly sometimes, but that we generally muddle forward and prevail. Editors of environmental regionals are producing articles that ultimately address themselves to prevailing. The species that is endangered *can* make a comeback. Resources *can* be renewed. The environment *can* be saved. If editors didn't believe that, they wouldn't bother working on publications that address themselves to regions of this planet, their betterment and future.

But the editors do believe all that. And if you do, too, you should be writing for regional environmental publications. Spread the good news.

12

Take 'em By the Hand

Writing city and country guidebooks

The regional publications which are most notably chauvinistic about their pieces of the world are guides and tour books. Positive publications are affirmative about their regions but the guides and tour books are unequivocally so. Positive publications appeal to readers who, for one reason or another, left the region they love; they appeal to—and play up to—folks who are homesick. Guides and tour books are aimed at newcomers, visitors, and tourists. "You're here and we want you to enjoy your stay," they say. "We want you to talk about us when you go home again. And we want you to return."

And so guides and tour books sing an unabashedly sanguine song. If you're going to write for one, plan to border on the giddy. No need to tell untruths. *Vermont Life* publishes an annual guide and has never utterd a fib in its pages. On the other hand, we have never run a *Guide* article on the discomforts of black flies in June. We also tend to downplay the fact that in Vermont, the season of spring occasionally lasts up to a week and a half, but those days seldom run concurrently.

Similarly, a San Francisco tour guide may suggest you pack an umbrella in May (rather than telling you that you would be a damned fool not to). The tour guide describing Harbor Island in the Bahamas doesn't whisper a word about the lizards or the litter, though there are plenty of both. When Martin Fischhoff wrote "The Look Homeward Angle: A Guide to Writing City Guidebooks" (*Writer's Digest*, December, 1978) he described the discretion of a guidebook editor with this eloquence: "There's no town so dull, so parochial, so beyond redemption that it doesn't deserve or can't support a guide book. I should know. I wrote one on Detroit."

Fischhoff financed his seemingly impossible literary venture himself and pocketed $12,000 from his year's gross sales. Other state or city guides and tour books are financed by supporting agencies. But whether public or private, they essentially differ very little in tone. And the tone is a sweet one indeed.

Tour guides can be published annually—as are the *New England Guide*, *Vermont Life's Guide to Vermont* and *Denver Tours*. Annual guides have the advantage of being for sale for twelve months, but normally the sale is limited to season. If a guide carries advertising or a calendar of events, a year would be its maximum life before it became outdated. Some guides, which carry neither, are valid for their regions for indefinite periods of time. Others, like *Brown's Guide to Georgia* and *Santa Cruz* magazine in California, are monthly guides with very specific information about who is appearing in what nightclub and who is preaching in what church. The number of times a guide is issued dictates its immediacy but a single city guide with no dates and no commericals could be useful and salable for many years.

Guides can be narrowed in scope. *Vermont Life* produces guides to the inns of Vermont, to the lakes of Vermont and the theaters of Vermont. You might want to think of a guide in your region for young people, or offer a guide to historic

sites, craft shops and—especially for foreign visitors—
factories that accept tours. Be inventive. If people come to
visit your area, you should be able to come up with a way that
will make their visit more pleasurable and profitable.

When you come up with your guide idea, unless you have
capital that you're itching to part with, it makes sense to find
a sponsor. Chambers of commerce are the most obvious
places to find seed money, but by no means the only place.
Any organization that is dependent upon or interested in the
tourist business could be interested in sponsoring a tourist
promotion. There are also publishers, smaller than major
book houses but large enough to handle the production of a
guide, and their owners might be interested in gambling on
your product's salability.

Vachon's (and nearly everyone else's) Law of Success
states: The gamble pays off if your product brings in more
money than it cost to produce.

Many private guide publishers who sell advertising space
will set an advertising/editorial ratio that insures that the
product will pay for itself even if not one single copy is sold.
The ads carry the whole production load, and that's pretty
smart business. If you print 10,000 guides and sell them for
$3 apiece, less 40 percent for the retailer and 10 percent for
the wholesaler, you've made $15,000 for some very pleasant
work. If you skip the middlemen, the amount doubles rather
nicely. (Guides generally sell for significantly under $10
depending on the color they carry and the amount of pages
they fill. Color is expensive and, with the exception of the
cover, unnecessary.)

On the cover, color—and a bright, simple, attractive
picture or design—is crucial. Pick something that will sell
itself, something that will leap off the shelf and shout "Buy
Me!" Add cover copy telling would-be buyers what lies
between the covers. And put the name of your guide in large
bold letters. ("They can be any color at all," says magazine
consultant Peter Sykas of Edmonton, Washington, "as long
as the color is red.") Be sure to fill your guide with visuals.

Take you reader by the hand and walk him through town (or county or whatever you're providing the tour of). You can get free photographs for the asking from your state information or travel division. Maps are generally available from your local highway department office, county surveyor, and U.S. Geologic Survey office, and while you had better find their policy in republishing them, you will almost certainly find more cooperation than most people would have the right to expect.

Stay away from indifferent-quality drawings in guides if a good photograph can be obtained to do the same job more accurately. Amateurish line drawings announce that a guide was done amateurishly and tourists aren't interested in advice from amateurs.

Especially if you plan to finance your own guide, make certain you aren't duplicating someone else's efforts and if you discover that you *are*, make certain your efforts are going to be superior. (At *Vermont Life*, we knew that at least three other guides were being published that covered Vermont but because no one was giving the Green Mountain State exclusive treatment, we decided to move in. If we were given serious competition from a new publication, we would gracefully bow out.)

You might want to create a mock-up of a city guide before sinking too much money into your own venture. Find a printer in your city and ask for some production estimates. You might go to several printers and get competitive bids. Tell each bidder exactly what you have in mind. For example:

Trim size—8½ inches by 11 inches
Pages—128
Full page black and white photos—32
Full color cover
Press run—10,000 copies
Advertising/editorial ratio—50/50

The bidders will probably ask some other questions to make

sure they know all the expenses they might incur and then, if they want the business, you'll know how much your guide will cost to produce.

Your next step should be to determine the costs of distributing and promoting the guide and also to establish whether local news dealers and bookstores will carry it and what discount they will require. (Simple task, that: merely ask.) When you've determined how much it will cost to produce, promote and distribute your guide, think about advertising. You might go to an advertising agency for expertise, or you might turn the entire account over to them. "I plan to publish a tour guide of Toledo," you might say to your friendly local adman. "It will cost $20,000 to print 10,000 copies and so if I sold them at $2 and sold every one, I'd break even. But since it's unlikely I'll have a complete sellout in this, my first year of operation, and since breaking even is hardly my motive in this venture to begin with, I'd like to fill about half this Guide with advertisements. Can you give me a hand?"

For about 15 percent of the handle, if the agency thinks you have a viable product, they will be happy to give you a hand. And it's a good hand to have. Not only can the agency help aesthetically to keep your guide's advertising layout and copy out of the atrocity file, it can also ease your editoral conscience. The guide entepreneurs who find themselves in the most difficulty are those who try to handle both the advertising and editorial end of their product. They find conflict is inevitable. "Certainly, we would be delighted to take a full page ad in your guide. And we know you're anxious to run an article in it on our amazing Mr. Maurice—a magician with a razor cut and a positive genius with a blow dryer." That kind of aggravation you don't need.

If you are writing the tour guide yourself, you should be getting all the free help you can get. (Also, in preparing a guide book, you should take into account Hofstadter's Law which first appeared in the pages of Omni and is attributed to Douglas Hofstadter of Bloomington, Indiana. It goes like this:

"It always takes longer than you expect, even when you take Hofstadter's Law into account.") The chamber of commerce might be near the top of your list of contributors. If they don't have a guide of their own—and if they don't perceive you as being the competition—their members ought to be extremely good to you. After all, you're trying to promote business and that's the chamber's only reason for being. (You're also probably trying to make a profit for yourself and you might even be secretly thinking about what it will look like to see the word "editor" after your name. But where was it ever stated that you have to bare *all* the secrets of your soul to the chamber of commerce?)

As a general rule, a tour guide should contain the following features:

One: A guide to restaurants, with visits to the known and the unusual. List outstanding characteristics, price ranges and anything else you think would be helpful to a visitor looking for a place to have dinner. Are families welcome? That's important to know. Is there a waiting list on weekends? Reservations preferred? What credit cards are accepted? Give insider's tips: the name of the sommelier, and how much to tip the captain. Tell your readers about the table in the rear with the view of the waterfall, or the eat-in, take-out delicatessen with pastrami on pumpernickel and special mustard that tastes like it was made in heaven.

Two: A guide to bars. Bars are places to meet people and a city tour guide would be performing a helpful service by warning or clarifying what the normal clientele is. It might also be useful to tell your readers that at lunch, the bartender goes pretty heavy on the tabasco in Bloody Marys or that the house scotch is Ballantine's.

Three: A shopping guide. Give your readers diversity. They'll know about the department stores, and won't be able to miss them even if they don't. But is there an unusual import shop hidden on a side street somewhere? Are prices better on one side of town than another? Is there a leather tanner who sells goods from his barn and can you see the raw materials grazing on his hillside? Give details. Make certain everyone knows *you* are an authority.

Four: A guide to the arts. The local Council on the Arts usually has a full calendar of events available for the asking, and people who work for it can recommend what is most worth a visit. The Shakespeare Festival may be sub-par this year and the Children's Mime Troupe superb.

Five: A guide to sporting events. Tell visitors about events worth watching, participating in, or avoiding. Keep on top of running, hiking, and cycling events that are open to the public, and cockfights and casinos that are not. List the best public jogging courses, golf courses, and bike trails.

Six: A guide to special attractions. List the zoos and museums and unusual churches—but don't stop there. A section on unpublicized sights should be as long or longer than the predictable ones, if you have done your research.

A comprehensive guide should tell a traveler where the best campsites are located, where the private campgrounds are found, what the fishing and hunting rules and fees are, where to find country stores or antique shops, gift shops and wildlife preserves. Natural attractions, such as Virginia's Natural Bridge or Yellowstone's Old Faithful, should be touted, but does the region you are guiding folks through also have a castle open to visitors? A gondola to take riders to the top of a nearby mountain? Are there ships or ferries to be taken, a farmer's cooperative to be toured, a mine that can be examined or a national historic site to be savored? A guide containing too much information is more useful than one containing too little. Don't skimp on the facts: tourists want to know all there is to know about your area. They want to cram as much into as short a period of time as possible.

The *best* source of information about a city is its residents—your fellow city-dwellers. It's generally true that if people like living in their town, visitors will like visiting there.

But remember, you are not only guiding visitors with your tour guide, you are reinforcing their fantasies. When people come to Vermont for the first time, they expect to see dirt roads, covered bridges, picturesque villages, frugal farmers, and general stores. They don't expect to see factory towns, trailer parks, or shopping malls. Vermont has plenty of the former and plenty of the latter. The tour guide promotes the former.

I offer no apologies. Nor should you if your tour guide of Seattle plays up the marinas on Lake Washington but scoots past the canneries on First Avenue. Or if your Providence tour guide sings the praises of downtown renovation but ignores the suburban sprawl that stretches up Route TK all the way to Boston. Surely you will be forgiven if your Annual Guide to the New Jersey Shore dawdles in Spring Lake and Tom's River but ducks rapidly through Long Branch and Red Bank.

But while you're writing all this enthusiastic, positive prose, be careful not to be gushy or exaggerated. You can't fool any of the people any of the time if you call all the restaurants "superb, clean, friendly, and fast." All the bars aren't "neighborhood pubs that feature relaxed ethnic local color." There *are* dull museums, and if you guide someone to one under false pretenses, you will have lost a customer for next year.

Rather than speak in generalities and stereotypes, aim for the highest possible degree of specificity. Don't say "the cuisine is excellent." Say, "you might try the Coquille St. Jacques." (But right before press time, make certain Pierre has not been replaced by Mario in the kitchen.) The way to really come off like an expert is to get specific and back up generalizations with facts.

If you are reviewing restaurants, inns, diners, hotels, pizza or tatto parlors—or anything else that might deserve a review—set up an objective system for grading. You might plan to rate from one to 25 on food, atmosphere, service, and price. When you print your review, publish the breakdown of your grading. (If you merely marked a restaurant "16," for example, and didn't mention that the atmosphere, service, and price were superb but you were hospitalized with severe ptomain only hours after your last visit there, people could get the wrong impression and flock to the place in record numbers. An epidemic is a difficult thing to carry on your conscience.)

You'll find that as you are gathering information for a city guide, most restaurants, attractions, and motels are going to be unusually courteous. Their proprietors realize only too well what a bad review disseminated to thousands of tourists could do for their businesses. In preparing his guide to Detroit, Fischhoff says he only once got turned down for a free meal. The restaurant's owner rejected him because he had spent the previous year eating free meals in New York and saying he was writing a guide book. It had been a little fib. (If I were writing a guide book of Detroit, I would never tell an owner in advance that I was coming to his restaurant nor would I reveal my mission once there. I suspect I'd lose a lot of money that way, but I would also see typical service and eat typical food. Maybe I'm being overzealous.)

One delightful way to show the inherent character of a town—which the AAA and chamber of commerce publications generally fail to do—is to pack your copy with human interest stories. Find the folks who breathe life into your region—the 80-year-old doctor who is still practicing; the 12-year-old speed skater with Olympic aspirations, the farmer turned businessman or the businessman turned farmer. Find a haunted house, an odd characteristic of a city, the unpublicized attractions, the eccentric architecture. Find the unusual, the off-the-beaten-track restaurant, the unknown botanical garden—the "insider's" view. Make the reader of your guide feel like he's marching to a slightly different drummer than are all the rest of the city's tourists, and give him a slightly different beat.

"What makes a tour guide sell is being *beneath* the scenes and speaking straightforwardly," Fischhoff warns. If a tourist feels that the guide can offer more than the AAA can give, it will be a financial winner.

Tour guides must be written precisely but quickly. Information gets outdated, says Vachon's Law of the Annual Guide, in direct proportion to its prominence in print. The restaurant you featured in color is more likely to go out of business, change ownership or burn to the ground than the gift shop you featured in black and white. The nut shop you ignored altogether shall prosper and multiply.

Never send a finished tour guide to the printer without going over all the facts one final time. If you have to kill an article and are suddenly faced with three empty pages, you will have absolutely no trouble filling them in one day. The local chapters of the American Cancer Society, Heart Fund, and United Way would be more than willing to give you camera-ready art. Free.

Finally, when you are putting together a guide book for your city or region, add a touch of timelessness. If you have a calendar of events (taking up a major section in your editorial content), your guide is good for a year only. But if the events are included as a separate pamphlet that can be exchanged for a new one annually, the guide will have a longer life. Then maybe you *will* sell all 10,000 in print. There's money in them there numbers.

Tour guides require expertise, flair, specifics, and facts. Put all that together, and any city can be a wonderful town, any region a tourist's delight. Make yourself indispensable to a visitor and you'll make yourself some money.

13

That's No Article, That's a Book

How and where to sell it

When photographer Clyde Smith walked into the offices of Viking Press with a book concept in his mind and a stash of pictures under his arm, it was obvious he was no native of Madison Avenue. His hiking boots, jeans, and flannel shirt didn't harmonize with predominant wardrobian theme—Brooks Brothers and Lord & Taylor, with just a touch of L.L. Bean. Smith didn't even *smell* like he belonged. The faintly unwholesome odor of insect repellent had not completely been eliminated for this trip to New York City.

But he was determined, admittedly he says today, because he didn't know any better. He was an architect-turned-photographer who had been living in the Adirondacks for several years, and he thought it was about time somebody did a book on that upper New York State wildlife area. He had been contributing photographs to the regional magazine *Adirondack Life* for some time, but had been selling only first rights. Once they were published their ownership reverted to Smith, and on this particular day Smith's possessions were in his portfolio, ready to be shown off.

At first, no one was eager to do much looking. Smith may have looked right for the part—rugged good looks and Adirondack attire—but any junior editor at a major publishing house knows you don't talk book to someone right off the street. Any publishing secretary knows that you don't make appointments for the boss with a photographer. At the very most, an appointment might be arranged with the photographer's agent. If that agent has a good reputation and a solid track record.

"But *I* didn't know any of that," Smith recalls. "So I just kept going to one person after another—I think they passed me off to about eight people—and finally I get to talk with someone. He thumbs through my portfolio and says he thinks the photographs look interesting.

"Then he throws the bomb at me. 'Who's going to write this book?' he says.

" 'What's it going to need?' I ask him.

" 'About 20,000 words,' he says.

"So I said I guess I'd better do it.

"We talked some more and eventually I signed a contract."

The Adirondacks was published a year later. Smith has also provided photographs for the regional books *New England, New England Coast, New York,* and *Pennsylvania,* published by Graphics Arts Publishing Company in Portland, Oregon. He is undoubtedly one of the most successful regional photographers around. He has the talent but he also had the luck. Someone at Viking was willing to sit down and look at what he had to offer. But that is a brand of luck writers shouldn't count on. Our skills are less obvious, and we may have to push them harder.

Regional books are getting published more and more frequently and the reception for them has been outstanding. Smith's *New England,* which was written by Anne Glickman, a public relations director in Cambridge, Massachusetts, is currently in its third printing. Smith gets about $4 for every book that is sold. Not bad.

Living Better in Cincinnati by Lois Rosenthal (Writer's Digest Books) sold out its first printing of 10,000 copies. *The Mississippi Cookbook* (University Press of Mississippi) has sold over 28,000 copies as of this writing, and *Adobe–Build It Yourself* by P.G. McHenry (University of Arizona Press) is in its seventh printing. And these are random examples— there are hundreds more.

When is a magazine article clearly something with book potential? Mostly, when you have more to say than a magazine can carry, and when what you have to say can sustain interest.

That happened to me in 1972 when I returned to New York after covering the Jesus Movement in California. *Look* magazine had sent me to cover the phenomenon taking root along the Pacific Coast that was turning thousands of young people on to old-time religion.

When I returned from a week-long assignment, I locked myself inside a *Look* office, gathered all my notes, and knocked off 4,000 words in ten hours. It was hard, grueling work because I was excited about what I had seen in California and wanted to accurately convey that excitement. I wrote draft after draft, and finally I had what I wanted.

I brought my manuscript into the office of *Look* managing editor Martin Goldman, deposited it on his desk, and pluncked myself on a nearby sofa. "I think you're going to like it," I said.

"I hope so," Goldman said. "We didn't send you to California to improve your tan." An aristocrat of editors, Goldman was not above traces of sarcasm.

"What are you doing here?" he said to me.

"I'm waiting for you to read my manuscript," I said, stifling the "what do you think I'm doing here, basking in the warm rays of your personality?"

He became, for Goldman, almost tender. "Vachon, I will read your precious piece this evening. Right now, I have a minor obligation. I have a magazine to get out. Now beat it.

We can talk about it tomorrow."

It was not a short evening, the one that followed. I think a major flaw in all us writers is that we need immediate feedback. We need someone *else* to say "Oh, that was very good," or "sorry, that was pretty dreadful," before we can place a value judgment on something we've written. And then we invariably adopt that someone else's values as our own. So seldom do we say about something we composed: "This is good stuff. I know it is good and no one will convince me otherwise." That kind of confidence would be a great asset to a writer.

One I certainly didn't have the next day when I sidled into Martin Goldman's office for his verdict on my Jesus Movement piece.

"Sit down," he indicated.

I sat.

"It gives me considerable pain to say this to you, Vachon," I felt my body begin to flinch. "but this is good."

"Oh?" I brightened.

"In fact it's awfully good. And three times too long."

"Three times too. . . ."

"Go cut it down," Goldman said. "And don't you dare cut out the best stuff."

I took the manuscript and went home to my Upper West-Side apartment. Three times too long! What could go? How on earth was I going to cut 3,000 words from a 4,000-word piece?

I didn't know it at the time, but a book was being born. Those 4,000 words would eventually become 60,000, became *A Time to Be Born*, published by Prentice-Hall.

For that evening, though, I cut. It was far more painful and time-consuming than the writing had been. When I handed my expurgated version to Goldman the next day, he was clearly pleased and I was vaguely dissatisfied. I had more to say and wanted a platform from which to say it. A month or so later, an agent was keeping appointments with publishers, presenting my prospectus for a book.

Vague dissatisfaction may not be the failsafe signal that indicates a magazine article can be stretched or shaped or prodded into a book; but it's not a bad early warning sign. Another is interest. Do you have something fascinating or important or funny enough to sustain interest level forty or fifty times as long as it takes to read an average magazine article? If you had difficulty meeting your editor's suggested 2,000 words, you will go absolutely out of your mind when you try to take on something as hefty as a book. But if you feel that you are bubbling with things that need to be said, get that query letter and chapter sample off to a book publisher. If you have more information on a subject than any reasonably well-occupied regional magazine editor would even consider plowing through—but if you think it has true value—you've got a book.

Consider What Sells

While many regional magazines can be sustained without realizing a profit—because they are bankrolled by agencies whose overall vested interest is promoted by the publication—no publisher of regional books is so motivated (with the exception—sometimes—of university presses, discussed later). They *have* to make money or they don't survive. When you are considering a regional book, consider it first as a product that must sell a certain number before it makes a profit. That is precisely how your potential publisher will judge it.

"Writing books is simply a business venture," says Charles Allyn of the Great Outdoors Publishing Company in St. Petersburg, Florida. "Writers have to write what sells. No matter how well a book is written and no matter what it means to the author, if it isn't going to sell it shouldn't be published."

That's not being harsh: it's simply being practical.

Book Markets

Book publishers come in all sizes and some may be more

compatible with your project than others. On the high end of the scale are the likes of *Random House, Simon and Schuster, Doubleday,* and *Prentice-Hall.* They are the heavy hitters, interested in a regional book only if it has very good selling possibilities.

John Kirk, editor-in-chief of Prentice-Hall, had this rule of thumb when considering a book with a regional flavor: it must sell 10,000 copies in its first year of existence. He didn't care *where* those 10,000 books were sold. The scope of sales wasn't part of his rule, only the number. *The Wildflowers of Walla Walla,* would interest Kirk if all the evidence indicated that 10,000 Walla Wallingtonians would snap the volume up within twelve months of its publication date.

Of course, he would be *gambling* that wildflowers in southern Washington would be that compelling a subject. There is no real guarantee that *any* book is going to sell 10,000 copies in one year (Irving Wallace novels and gothics with "lust" in the title being the only immediate exceptions). With the big market publishers, though, you have to present a mighty compelling case for your subject matter. You're going to have to prove that your treatment of a region, or a feature of a region, is going to have market appeal.

A second level of publishing includes smaller publishing houses that have national distribution potential. Charles Belding of Portland, Oregon, whose Graphic Arts Center Publishing Company specializes in regional books, says that he is looking for books that have the strongest possible visual appeal. Orion Barber of the Stephen Greene Press in Brattleboro, Vermont, will consider a regional book only if he sees a national potential.

"I live in New England and am an editor of a New England publishing house. So naturally the regionals I will see have a New England flavor," says Barber. "But that book, if we're going to get interested in it, also has to find people who don't live in New England any more but who have ties here. The book has to appeal to people who have New England in their hearts. If we just depended on regional sales for regional books, we'd be out of business.

"The bottom line for the publisher has to be the bottom line in our financial report. No matter how much we love a region, as publishers, we have to love it with practicality."

Bob Friedman of the Donning Company publishers of Norfolk, Virginia, suggests that writers write for as broad a market as possible. "Publishing companies generally won't publish on esoteric subjects geared for an equally esoteric audience. It doesn't make financial success."

The editors at Viking agree. "To be profitable, a book has to be of more than just local interest," says one. "Successful books on local or specific regions must strike a balance between particular and universal. Choose a specific subject but make it come alive for all readers, including those unfamiliar with the region. One way to do this is to go beneath the surface. A stuffy museum, for example, can come alive when the scandalous or humorous tales of its past occupants are recited."

Bob Friedman warns writers not to handicap their own book's salability. "For example, if you have a recipe which contains an ingredient only available in a specific region, try to come up with viable alternatives for that ingredient for those who may live outside the region."

Peter Jennison, publisher of the Countryman Press in Taftsville, Vermont, puts out several regional books each year and has learned from mistakes as well as from successes.

"Regional titles are rarely sold much outside the region they represent," he believes. "For this reason, they must retain a perennial rather than a topical appeal. If the book has value as a reference book or resource for research, then it will sell in three or four years as well as it will the first.

"But writers should avoid faddish topics in regional books because the market is small enough as it is."

Jennison feels that nostalgia books are shrinking in readership but that books on crafts and skills of an earlier society can usually sell well. If a book can be used as a high school text or reference and also appeal to a general regional audience, that's all the better.

The middle level of publishing house can't afford to take a gamble with a book notion that might have potential. Big publishing houses won't, and middle publishing houses can't. You're more likely to find someone in the remaining levels of the industry who's willing to shoot craps in the hopes of making a killing on a particular book.

The remaining levels of book publishing contain the "literary and little" book publishers scattered around the country that operate on a shoestring (and pay authors accordingly); the university presses; and non-book publishers that happen to publish books.

The rules of the game are a bit different for university presses than for other publishing houses. Many of these are at least partly subsidized by the universities with which they are affiliated and were established for the altruistic purpose of publishing books on the basis of merit rather than marketability. That doesn't mean the university presses aren't looking to pick up a buck here and there; most depend on the fat, juicy profits from one or two big sellers in order to be able to publish another book that they know will lose money and be read by only a handful of college professors.

The good news is that most of the eighty-odd university presses in the U.S. just love to publish regional books. Their marketing departments are better prepared to sell books on a regional than a national level (although a university press book does make the *New York Times* best-seller list once in a while), and they consider the preservation of the history and culture of their states and regions a big part of their noble cause. The bad news is that few of them can sell as many copies of your book as a big trade publisher can. So don't go to a university press with a manuscript you can market on Madison Avenue.

But the book you have in mind to write *could* be only a marginal book—which could easily have a local market. *A Guide to Savannah Cemeteries* might not be the book the world is waiting for, but it would sell some copies. *The Idaho*

Falls Guide to Country Inns won't hit the best-seller list, but it's going to sell in Idaho Falls. *A Taste of Old Madison: Collected Recipes and Nostalgia from Madison's Old Days* sold almost 5,000 copies in Madison, Wisconsin.

You might have a potentially top-selling book, and publishers aren't going to sneer at those possibilities. But as a writer, you have to tailor your writing to a publisher's outlets, audience, and possibilities. Don't go to Doubleday with *New Hampshire's Round Barns* when Rumford National Graphics, Inc., in Concord would be infinitely more interested.

Books are also published outside of book publishing houses. Museums, historical societies, and magazine publishers crank out a volume now and then. *Vermont Life* put out a book called *Vermont: A Special World* in 1969. We hoped that it would eventually sell out its 15,000 first printing. It's currently in its sixth printing, has sold over 60,000 copies, and is largely responsible for *Vermont Life's* financial independence. We gambled and won.

But our gamble was a fairly modest one. Almost all the photographs that appeared in *Vermont: A Special World* had previously appeared in *Vermont Life*, so the high cost of color separations was eliminated. Since the book was written by staff, there was no royalty to pay. Since the book was assembled on state time by state employees, the overhead was minimal. Since the book was assembled with a paper stock our printer had in abundant supply, the publishing costs were kept low. In all, the book cost just under $4 to produce and we retailed it for $15. We sold it for approximately four times as much as it cost to make.

Private enterprise publishers could never operate in a four-to-one ratio. Their overhead costs are much too high, and they operate on a ratio closer to seven-to-one. Remember that fact when you are planning a volume of wonderful words. If a publisher thinks it will cost him $4 to put all your wonderful words inside a hardcover book, he has to plan to sell that book for about $28 a copy. That had better be one heck of a good book!

The Subsidy Press

Any company that advertises nationally that it will publish your book without costing you a dime is either a fraud or a philanthrophy. If you have lots of money to fritter away, and an ego that needs plenty of stroking, subsidy—or "vanity" publishers—are right for you. They *will* publish your memoirs or a collection of your poetry or your essays on truth in all its aspects. But you'll pay for every page of every book, every hour of every pressman, deliveryman, production supervisor; you'll pay for every drop of ink, for binding and packaging. And then you will pay an additional percentage to the subsidy publisher for the kindness shown to you in the first place.

If you must buy the right to be published, at least go in with your eyes open. Make certain you know in advance what the total price will be for a specific number of volumes, and get that in writing; and prepare for the fact that you will be doing all the promotion and selling for the book. Then get out your checkbook. And your handkerchief.

Indulge in subsidy publishing only if you have the willingness and ability to play a major role in the development, publicity, and sale of the book, and only if you have the available cash. Don't remortgage your house to finance the publishing of your grandfather's memoirs.

Closing the Deal

Among eternal questions in the literary world, one that hangs heaviest over the head of an author looking for a publisher, is the question of quantity. How much has to be done on pure speculation before the big boys will take the tops off their pens and put something in writing? How much is enough to start talking about advances and percentages and promotions? When is someone else going to take a stake in this book?

Like the majority of eternal questions, these have no simple or complete answers. I know some authors who have books published only after they have completed them. They've gone ahead and written an entire manuscript without being graced by a kind word from a publisher. That takes optimism and perseverence which slips well beyond the realm of my own understanding.

There are other authors who get huge advances for books that are just in the talking stage. James Michener, the ultimate regional book writer (Tales of the South Pacific, Chesapeake, Hawaii, etc.) does not have to submit sample chapters and outlines to his publisher before he get some front money. More likely, he will say to his agent, "I think I'll go south this winter." At his Florida address a few months later, he'll get a check for $100,000 and a year after that, Keys will be number one on the best-seller list.

There's only one James Michener. If you are a writer with decently established credentials—that is, someone who has published on a fairly regular basis in magazines of reasonable repute—a book publisher could fairly ask you for a full outline and a chapter to consider before contract time. If you are unpublished and unknown, publishers are going to be less likely to take a gamble on your offerings.

A writer also has to be able to sell himself. "Avoid both modesty and pushiness," Allyn advises. "We aren't particularly impressed by a name or past credentials. We aren't fooled; manuscripts speak for themselves.

Virtually all book publishers agree the worst mistake a writer can make—the biggest clue of amateurity he can offer—is a book of an autobiographical nature. (Precisely why the narration of this book has been so studiously omniscient.) "Avoid self-centered narratives," says one regional book editor. "A book on canning should not center on your life as a canner. This is an amateur's attempt at immortality. It should be about canning."

The second biggest mistake, say the publishers, is uneven writing. "You see it all the time," says an editor at Random House. "The manuscript will start out just great and then fizzle out after fifty pages or so. Writers have to capture their readers and hold them the whole way through."

At Viking, they prefer whole manuscripts to just excerpts for just this reason. "An excerpt can be deceptive. We want to know that the book is as solid in the last ten pages as it is in the first ten," an editor explained. "We read manuscripts for as long as they are fascinating. If the lead is stodgy or slow, you've lost us already.

Sometimes a piece of writing that is far too long for a magazine article is too short to be sustained as a book. That is a not-quite-book, and there is a place for them. Many regionals, most notably the *New Yorker*, publish in installments. Very long articles and essays get broken up into more easily digestible parts. Writers should never artificially stretch material to give it book length. Write it thoroughly and concisely. Then judge what it is after it's complete. If it's book length, sell it to a publisher. Anything less than 20,000 words is probably not a book.

Bob Friedman at Donning Company says writers might help themselves by doing a little prepublication marketing themselves. "If a writer has viable places to market the book, by doing a little pre-selling himself and by going to various organizations and drumming up some interest, and he mentions this in his query, his chances of acceptance are greater. If an unknown author has lined up a market for a book and is willing to assume responsibility for the sales, so much the better." Friedman warns that this advice will help only in borderline acceptance/rejection cases. And it won't necessarily help at all in the major publishing houses.

Finally, Friedman gives some advice that I find interesting. He says writers might run into success by calling book publishers and editors on the phone, citing past credentials, and asking if there is any topic that needs covering. "Frequently editors get a mountain of manuscripts on one subject and none on a topic they've been chewing on a while. A polite inquiry from a past published writer shows initiative. Also, the editor will be receptive to the idea from the start since it was his to begin with."

If the property you have or the book you want to write is worthwhile, you'll find a publisher eventually. Be persistant. And don't be too fussy about advance money. An advance is absolutely what the name implies and nothing more. It's not a bonus like professional athletes receive. It's an advance against royalties. It is the gamble the publisher is willing to make on your writing. It will be subtracted from your royalties when they begin coming in. (Royalty percentages are generally between ten and fifteen percent, beginning at the low figure and advancing up with additional printings. Each printing costs a publisher less and so the author is deserved of more.)

Publishers of regional books seem fussier about neatness—much more so than editors of regional magazines. They like neat, accurate manuscripts and could be turned off by typing crossovers, sloppy proofreading, and even smudged paper. Make your package as neat and presentable as possible and you increase your chances considerably. Remember also that first-person intrusions are not appreciated by regional book publishers. Magazine publishers often find the vertical pronoun a welcome addition to a story, but book publishers see "I" as a label of inexperience and ineptness.

Choosing a Book Topic

With any potential topic, ask yourself these questions:

Is there a need for a book on this subject? Check in the bookstores and libraries (*Subject Guide to Books in Print* is available in most) and make certain your proposed book really does fill an existing void.

Who is going to buy your book, and why? If you can't choose a specific and diverse group of people who are likely to buy your book, choose another topic. Don't waste your time or a publisher's with a great idea that nobody's interested in. Pinpoint your audience. A history of Silver City, New Mexico, may be charming and chock full of lovable characters. But who, besides a handful of local residents and some larger state libraries, would want to buy the book? The topic you choose must be broad enough to interest more than a handful of people.

"Consider your audience," says Charles Allyn of Great Outdoors Publishing Company. "Boston suburbia? Vermont farmer? Dallas businessman? Write using their educational comprehension level and their interests."

You must be perceptive about which way the wind is blowing. Good timing is essential.

An editor of the Stephen Greene Press in Brattleboro tells this story:

"A few number of years ago we received a manuscript about cross-country skiing in New England. At the time, the sport was unpopular with most people, yet the topic intrigued us. With the high cost of downhill skiing, we saw real possibilities for increased popularity of the sport. So despite its off-beatness, we came out with the first book on cross-country skiing. The book went great guns and now the market is saturated with books on the subject."

Your book idea ought to be timely but it shouldn't be faddish. A book about Whittier, California, was worthless after Watergate, and a book about hoola hoops was worthless from its very inception. Books about Ohio, the Northeast, or the Southwest have a history of selling nicely. Books that lavish attention on the Midwest, the eastern central states and the Rockies tend not to do so well. (That is not a rule that defies breaking: it's simply an established pattern.)

Does the book fall into a category? Is it history, autobiography, or a travelogue?

A book with a good chance for making sales can be thematically regional. Southern cookbooks, for example, tend to make their publishers grin all the way to the barbeque pit. Collections of essays, on the other hand, don't do quite as well. Noel Perrin, author of *First Person Rural*, a collection of essays that previously appeared in the *New Yorker*, the *New York Times*, *Vermont Life*, and *Country Journal* received uniformly high praise from reviewers for his efforts. The book, however, was only mildly successful. It's a sad lesson to pass along: Noel Perrin, an English professor at Dartmouth College, is the best natural regional writer I know. But his book didn't sell very well. In the book business, skill doesn't necessarily translate into success and I'm sorry about that. In the book business, success is measured by mass appeal. And don't act so surprised. Does it shock you that ten times more people watch "Mork and Mindy" than watch "Masterpiece Theater"? And in the book business, we're talking to the same folks.

Are Agents Necessary?

Having an agent makes life simple. Agents let writers be writers and frees them from being promoters, accountants, dunners, and salesmen. Agents let writers be creative without worrying about the nuts and bolts that go into putting the subsequent creation on display.

Agents also have *entre* where writers often do not. Many publishers—including those that want to publish good regional books—want submissions from agents rather than authors. "When an agent gives me something to read, it at least tells me that one person has already reviewed it and liked it," one publisher told me. "The manuscript is less likely to be sloppy if it is presented by an agent. Agents won't let their writers hand in a sloppy manuscript. It costs them nothing to tell the writer to clean up his act. It might cost them plenty if the manuscript is a mess."

Agents take at least 10 percent of the profits of any writing venture. (Photographic agents take at least 40 percent.) That is their major disadvantage.

The second disadvantage is that the writer-agent relationship is characterized by a curious role reversal. Theoretically, if you hire an agent, that person is in your employ and is working for you. In reality, things don't work out that way.

You may be doing the lion's share of the work and you will—if the agent is successful—make the lion's share of the profits. But from the moment you strike a deal with an agent until the moment the book you struck a deal for is published, you will be working for him. He will call you early in the morning and ask you why he woke you up. He'll remind you of deadlines and hound you into meeting them.

Sometimes agents tell you how to dress, whom you can talk to, and even what to eat. If your agent is doing a good job for you, the best idea is to listen and obey. And if he isn't, fire him.

* * *

Turning an idea into a regional book is not easy. But it can be done, and if you have an idea that seems workable, you might as well be one of the writers who does it. The summary of suggestions that will place your idea between hard covers are these:

- Be an authority on your subject.
- Avoid self-centered writing.
- Write for a specific audience, and as broad a one as possible.
- Avoid rehashes and crowded markets. Fill a need with your book.
- Research thoroughly.
- Hand in only neat, accurate manuscripts.
- Follow the stands suggested in Writer's Market. Most publishers listed will suggest that you query; send sample chapters and/or synopsis; and always, return postage.

14

Expanding Your Markets

Regional refinements and recycling

Once you have sold a piece to a regional magazine, what are your chances of selling it again?

The answer to that question is either "none" or "plenty," depending on what kind of rights you sold to the original publisher.

At *Vermont Life*, we purchase first rights only. After your article has appeared in our pages, you can do whatever you want with it: resell it to your local newspaper, have an epic movie made out of it, turn it into a television mini-series, you name it. Because you own it. We relinquish all rights after the initial publication.

That's not quite as generous as it might sound. We buy first rights because we pay only ten cents a word. While that's not a paltry sum—most articles bring about $200 to the authors—it is a little on the low side. I don't feel we could maintain that rate and buy all rights. If *Vermont Life* publishes your article once and then wants to reprint it in a book, we pay a second fee.

Other magazines operate differently. Jerome Kelley, author of the informative *Magazine Writing Today*, found out the hard way. In his book, he discussed the background of writing an article for *Blair and Ketchum's Country Journal*. Then, to illustrate his points, he reprinted the article.

He shouldn't have. Kelley didn't own that article any more. *Country Journal* buys all rights to the material they purchase and the editors sent Kelley a bill for $200 for violating that understanding. The author was enormously surprised—he's a professional writer with hundreds of articles in print—and he simply forgot to inquire about rights. But he paid the bill, and admitted his oversight.

I was once thumbing through a magazine I had never seen before. It is called *Cleo* and it's published in Australia. Halfway through the glossy pages, I had quite a surprise of my own. There was a piece by me, with my name on it. I couldn't believe my eyes! How on earth could a magazine that I never even heard of publish an article of mine?

At the end of the article, I saw the explanation. In very fine print were the words "Copyright by *Ms.* Magazine." *Ms.* had published a piece of mine and then, because it owned all rights, sold it to *Cleo*. (I later learned that *Cleo* paid *Ms.* $300 for reprint permission. *Ms.* had originally paid me $200 for the article. Those women sure run some kind of business.)

The refrain that comes up again is familiar but no less valid for its repetition: When in doubt, ask. No editor will think any less of you for saying, "Pardon my ignorance, but what is your rights policy?" The editor would rather tell you now than explain after a misunderstanding.

Most regional magazines buy First North American Serial Rights. For example, if you were to sell a piece on historic buildings of Chicago's South Side to *Illinois* magazine, and gave that magazine First North American Serial Rights, you couldn't simultaneously sell it to *Chicago* magazine. You *could* sell it simultaneously to magazines in Tokyo or Calcutta—because they aren't in North America and *Illinois* has no control over what you do outside the continent.

Once *Illinois* prints your article, the rights—and owner-ship of it—revert to you. You can do with it what you will.

And what are your possibilities? In the United States, your options among other regionals are decidedly limited. *Chicago* isn't likely going to want to reprint something that has already appeared in *Illinois*. *Vermont Life* rarely picks up anything that has been published elsewhere. We like to think we're giving our readers something fresh, and most other regionals have the same policy.

But foreign publications pick up stories that appeared first in North America all the time. Germans are generally fascinated by Americans, for example, and if the South Side Chicago historic buildings you were writing about were owned or built or rented by Germans, you might be able to resell your article to *Bunte* or *Stern* or any of one of the other fine publications printed in West Germany. If the houses were filled with Englishmen, the *London Sunday Times* has a very handsome magazine, and its editor might be very interested in how those emigrants are comporting them-selves. If those historic houses were filled with Frenchmen, try *Paris Match*. And so on. Check *LMP* for names and addresses.

Foreign sales are real possibilities, even when the article originally written has no direct application to that foreign country. They like to see what we act like over here, especially when we're acting a bit peculiar. I once wrote a piece on witchcraft in San Francisco for the late *Look* magazine. My agent then sold it to three South American magazines and one West German one, and there wasn't a South American or a German mentioned in the whole piece. (There *was* some mention of nude coven meetings and tree-dwelling hermits and the First Church of Satan. Foreigners just eat that stuff up.)

"Hey, Pancho!"

"What is it, Henri?"

"Look what the crazy Americans are up to now."
"It figures."

You can expand your market in other ways, simply by thinking of your article as a piece of property that deserves to be exploited. First make sure it's yours to exploit. Some magazines assume all rights to an article unless otherwise stipulated. Make certain you know what your rights are. If a magazine offers less money for first-time rights than for all rights, make certain you're getting the best deal for you. If *New England*, the *Boston Globe* Sunday magazine, wanted to buy all rights to your story on an Arbor Day tree-planting ceremony in Cambridge, if I were you, I'd go ahead and sell them all rights. If, on the other hand, the *New York Times* Sunday magazine wanted to buy all rights to a penetrating and revealing interview you've just completed with Greta Garbo, I'd tell them I vanted them to go away.

You have to do a little bit of crystal-ball gazing with everything you write. What future potential does your writing have? The Arbor Day tree-planting ceremony was a specific event, exclusively American, and let's face it, a real yawner. There will never be a television situation comedy based on Boston kids planting balsams. Twentieth-Century Fox is never going to turn it into a monster. *Soviet Union Life* is not at all likely to ask for reprint rights to show how patriotic Americans help the ecology. So go ahead and sell the whole thing.

Now an interview with Greta Garbo is something else entirely. Since she hasn't granted an interview with any journalist for over forty years, and since she was once one of the most glamorous stars in Hollywood, if you did have an interview with her—and you won't—it would be worth a bundle.

Inexperienced photographers often make the mistake of selling negatives and transparencies to news organizations instead of simply selling first-time publication rights. There is always that amateur photographer at the airport who just happened to be pointing his camera at the sky when the stricken airplain began heading for a fatal crash. Will he sell his roll of film for $1,000? "My God! Those people were killed. A thousand dollars! For one little roll of film? My God!"

But odds being what they are, we're not likely to be at an airport photographing the sky when a plane is falling and we're not likely to be chosen by Garbo for her first interview in four decades. Our lives are made up of more predictable stuff. But that stuff can be expanded.

If you did an article for *Miami* magazine on the flora of Coral Gables, and if you provided the photographs, you could certainly make up a slide show later on to show to church groups and civic clubs. In my case, I have an intense aversion to speaking in public. Talking to more than three people at the same time fills me with dread. But because of my job, I occasionally can't avoid some public appearances. And the first words of every public address I ever give are "hit the lights." I show slides about how *Vermont Life* gets put together and in the darkened room, with those visual aids, my fear almost goes away.

If you don't have a similar aversion, you might look into the lecture circuit. It seems there's not a group in the world that doesn't have members vying for the title of program chairman. Speakers are always in demand, and if you have written an article that has been published by a regional publication, that makes you something of a celebrity in that region. If you let it be casually known that you are willing to speak to a garden club some day, don't be surprised if you get urgent phone calls from the Rotary, Kiwanis and Civitan clubs, the Jaycees and Jaycettes, American Leion and Veterans of Foreign Wars, the Boy Scouts, Girl Scouts, Bible Study Club, and the P.T.A. They'll all want to hear the speech.

One delightful part about that instant popularity is that the speech has almost been completely written. You and your regional editor have been working on it from the beginning. All your correspondence, first drafts, middle drafts, and last drafts can be parts of your speech. If there's a writer's club in your region, they will especially want you to speak. (Which is perfectly okay. But remember Rule Number Ten in Chapter Five. You can give speeches to writers' groups but don't hang around socializing too long after the meeting. Writers, as a group, have nothing to offer you. They'd pick your brain until it was clean, if you let them. Watch it.)

Your published article could be expanded into a film. If your words and the accompanying photographs were good enough to be published by a reputable regional, they probably are worth being animated. If you interviewed a 93-year-old gold prospectress for *Tulsa* magazine, I'd be willing to bet the Oklahoma Council on the Humanities would be willing to underwrite a filmed documentary on her life. If that Kansas wheat farmer you interviewed for *Focus/Midwest* was really as unique as you made him sound, you shouldn't have any trouble getting a documentary filmmaker to create something for your local educational television channel.

There are all kinds of ways to expand a single magazine article. Anyone working on a Foxfire-type book in your neck of woods these days? It's a rare neck if there isn't, and the editors of these educational publications are always looking for additional, pertinent material.

Could the magazine article you wrote be turned into a piece of fiction? You may not know what the Joy of Writing is all about until you have fictionalized your first story based on true events. It's absolutely a blissful experience. The research needed is minimal. And you never get stuck. You are limited only by your own imagination. When you are writing an article based on fact, you have to go with what is: When you're writing fiction, you work with what might be, what could be, and even what couldn't be. It's like playing God, only you get a check and a by-line.

The only problem with fiction is that most magazines in the regional field don't want it. Those of us who edit positive publications are accused too often of presenting a fictionalized, rosy version of our regions even when we expressly prohibit fiction. City magazine editors, whose reputations will fall and rise on their abilities to get the facts straight and get them out, have just as little use for the flights of your fancy.

There are some exceptions. *Yankee* publishes a great deal of fiction and pays well for the privilege. Most regionals associated with or sponsored by an educational institution will publish fiction but pay very little—if anything.

When in doubt, ask. When I get fiction in my morning mail, I shove it into its return envelope and get it off my desk as quickly as possible. It's an irritant. Fiction sent to *Vermont Life* has this implicit message: "Dear Person, I never bothered to look at your magazine. I don't care enough about it or you to take the time. Now, how about publishing a story of mine? My friends think it's terrific."

Then tell your friends to publish it. That's my reaction.

It is possible, however, to create some regional fiction and sell it to a nonregional market. The best way to expand your regional market is to go nonregional. And when you have done that, you have opened yourself up to every magazine that exists—thousands and thousands of them (16,000 in the United States, according to a reliable estimate).

Regional writing for nonregional publications is done all the time. My pieces in *Money*, the *New York Times*, *Delta Sky* (Delta's monthly magazine), *18 Almanac* (a Knoxville-based annual for young people leaving high school), *Sourcebook* (an annual for graduating seniors from that same Knoxville group that has purchased *Esquire*), *Esquire*, *Ford Times*, *Continental Odyssey* (a monthly for the Gulf Travel Club), and *Youth* (a Philadelphia-based monthly for church-related young people) have all been regional pieces. In most of them, I was writing about Vermont. In some of them, I was writing about New England. In one of them, I was writing about California. It didn't really make a great deal of difference. I was writing regional articles for general audiences. It works, and it pays.

Most of the rules that apply to regionals apply to nonregionals. Know the publication. Query first (even if the piece is written). Research diligently when necessary. Write deftly. Send neatly. Wait expectantly. If you have assembled a piece of writing that was soundly thought out and intelligently presented, you are going to sell it *somewhere*. Here are the fifteen types of publication open to you:

General Interest Publications
Reader's Digest, People, Life, and all the magazines that have no clearly limited audience or goal.

Science/Nature and Educational Magazines
Scientific American, National Wildlife, Psychology Today, and all the magazines that intend to inform.

Hobby and Leisure-time Activity Magazines
Anything about automobiles, airplanes, boating, cycling, diving, *Early American Life,* flower arranging, gardening, hiking, ice skating, jogging, karate, etc.

Ethnic Publications
Ebony, Jewish Post, I AM and every other magazine that cares about its readers' race and place of ancestral origin.

Religious Magazines
Sacred Heart Messenger, Baptist Life, Family Life magazine and every other magazine that cares about its readers' creed.

Cultural and Artistic Publications
Any publication covering the arts, movies, music, sculpture, television, etc.

Self-Improvement Magazines
Alternative life-styles, the occult, dieting, astrology, retirement living, etc.

Men's Magazines
From *Esquire* and *Playboy* to *Screw* and *Hustler*

Women's Magazines
Child care, education, food, home and garden, feminist issues, confession and gossip magazines, and every other magazine that *thinks* it's mostly for female persons.

Teen and Young Adult Publications
Thirteen- to 22-year-old audiences.
Juvenile Magazines
Humpty Dumpty and its ilk.
Little Magazines
Literary quarterlies, poetry, experimental writing.
Company/Union/Association Publications
House organs that get management's views across, union magazines that offer the other version, and club and fraternal magazines.
Trade, Technical, and Professional Journals
For retailers, manufacturers, undertakers, executives, doctors—there are more than 6,000 magazines in this field alone.
Miscellaneous Publications
Crossword puzzle magazines, science-fiction digests, and anything else that doesn't fall in the preceding fourteen categories.

It's a fairly impressive market out there. So what are you doing with a book in your hands? You should have typewriter keys under your fingers. You're a writer, aren't you?

Index

B

K

Books of Interest From Writer's Digest

Artist's Market, edited by Cathy Bruce and Betsy Wones. Contains over 3,000 commercial art buyers. Listings tell you who to contact and where, pay rates, special requirements and more. 432 pp. $10.95.

The Beginning Writer's Answer Book, edited by Kirk Polking, Jean Chimsky, and Rose Adkins. "What is a query letter?" "If I use a pen name, how can I cash the check?" These are among 567 questions most frequently asked by beginning writers—and expertly answered in this down-to-earth handbook. Cross-indexed. 270 pp. $8.95.

How to be a Successful Housewife/Writer, by Elaine Fantle Shimberg. The art of being a successful housewife/writer. 256 pp. $10.95.

The Cartoonist's and Gag Writer's Handbook, by Jack Markow. Longtime cartoonist with thousands of sales, reveals the secrets of successful cartooning—step by step. Richly illustrated. 157 pp. $8.95.

A Complete Guide to Marketing Magazine Articles, by Duane Newcomb. "Anyone who can write a clear sentence can learn to write and sell articles on a consistent basis." says Newcomb (who has published well over 3,000 articles). Here's how. 248 pp. $7.95.

The Confession Writer's Handbook, by Florence K. Palmer. A stylish and informative guide to getting started and getting ahead in the confessions. How to start a confession and carry it through. How to take an insignificant event and make it significant. 171 pp. $7.95.

The Craft of Interviewing, by John Brady. Everything you always wanted to know about asking questions, but were afraid to ask—from an experienced interviewer and editor of *Writer's Digest*. The most comprehensive guide to interviewing on the market. 244 pp. $9.95.

Craftworker's Market, edited by Lynne Lapin. Over 3,500 places for you to sell and exhibit your work. Listings include names and addresses, payment rates, special requirements and other information you need to sell your crafts. 696 pp. $11.95.

The Creative Writer, edited by Aron Mathieu. This book opens the door to the real world of publishing. Inspiration, techniques, and ideas, plus inside tips from Maugham, Caldwell, Purdy, others. 416 pp. $8.95.

The Greeting Card Writer's Handbook, by H. Joseph Chadwick. A former greeting card editor tells you what editors look for in inspirational verse...how to write humor...what to write about for conventional, studio and juvenile cards. Extra: a renewable list of greeting card markets. Will be greeted by any freelancer. 268 pp. $8.95.

A Guide to Writing History, by Doris Ricker Marston. How to track down Big Foot—or your family Civil War letters, or your hometown's last century—for publication and profit. A timely handbook for history buffs and writers. 258 pp. $8.50.

Handbook of Short Story Writing, edited by Frank A Dickson and Sandra Smythe. You provide the pencil, paper, and sweat—and this book will provide the expert guidance. Features include James Hilton on creating a lovable character: R.V. Cassill on plotting a short story. 238 pp. $9.95.

Law and the Writer, edited by Kirk Polking and Leonard S. Meranus. Don't let legal hassles slow down your progress as a writer. Now you can find good counsel on libel, invasion of privacy, fair use, taxes, contracts, social security, and more—all in one volume. 249 pp. $9.95.

Magazine Writing: The Inside Angle, by Art Spikol. Successful editor and writer reveals inside secrets of getting your mss. published. 288 pp. $10.95.

Magazine Writing Today, by Jerome E. Kelley. If you sometimes feel like a mouse in a maze of magazines, with a fat manuscript check at the end of the line, don't fret. Kelley tells you how to get a piece of the action. Covers ideas, research, interviewing, organization, the writing process, and ways to get photos. Plus advice on getting started. 220 pp. $9.95.

Mystery Writer's Handbook, by the Mystery Writers of America. A howtheydunit to the whodunit, newly written and revised by members of the Mystery Writers of America. Includes the four elements essential to the classic mystery. A comprehensive handbook that takes the mystery out of mystery writing. 273 pp. $8.95.

1001 Article Ideas, by Frank A. Dickson. A compendium of ideas plus formulas to generate more of your own! 256 pp. $10.95.

Writing for Regional Publications, by Brian Vachon. How to write for this growing market. 256 pp. $10.95.

One Way to Write Your Novel, by Dick Perry. For Perry, a novel is 200 pages. Or, two pages a day for 100 days. You can start and finish your novel, with the help of this step-by-step guide taking you from blank sheet to polished page. 138 pp. $8.95.

Photographer's Market, edited by Melissa Milar. Contains what you need to know to be a successful freelance photographer. Names, addresses, photo requirements, and payment rates for 3,000 markets. 624 pp. $12.95.

The Poet and the Poem, by Judson Jerome. A rare journey into the night of the poem—the mechanics, the mystery, the craft and sullen art. Written by the most widely read authority on poetry in America, and a major contemporary poet in his own right. 400 pp. $11.95.

Sell Copy, by Webster Kuswa. Tells the secrets of successful business writing. How to write it. How to sell it. How to buy it. 224 pp. $11.95.

Songwriter's Market, edited by William Brohaugh. Lists 2,000 places where you can sell your songs. Included are the people and companies who work daily with songwriters and musicians. Features names and addresses, pay rates and other valuable information you need to sell your work. 432 pp. $10.95.

Stalking the Feature Story, by William Ruehlmann. Besides a nose for news, the newspaper feature writer needs an ear for dialog and an eye for detail. He must also be adept at handling off-the-record remarks, organization, grammar, and the investigative story. Here's the "scoop" on newspaper feature writing. 314 pp. $9.95.

Successful Outdoor Writing, by Jack Samson. Longtime editor of *Field & Stream* covers this market in depth. Illustrated. 288 pp. $11.95.

A Treasury of Tips for Writers, edited by Marvin Weisbord. Everything from Vance Packard's system of organizing notes to tips on how to get research done free, by 86 magazine writers. 174 pp. $7.95.

Writer's Digest. The world's leading magazine for writers. Monthly issues include timely interviews, columns, tips to keep writers informed on where and how to sell their work. One year subscription, $15.

The Writer's Digest Diary. Plan your year in it, note appointments, log manuscript sales, be prepared for the IRS. It will become a permanent annual record of writing activity. Durable cloth cover. 144 pp. $8.95.

Writer's Market, edited by William Brohaugh. The freelancer's bible, containing 4,500 places to sell what you write. Includes the name, address and phone number of the buyer, a description of material wanted and rates of payment. 912 pp. $14.95.

The Writer's Resource Guide, edited by William Brohaugh. Over 2,000 research sources for information on anything you write about. 488 pp. $11.95.

Writer's Yearbook, edited by John Brady. This large annual magazine contains how-to-articles, interviews and special features, along with analyses of 500 major markets for writers. 128 pp. $2.50.

Writing and Selling Non-Fiction, by Hayes B. Jacobs. Explores with style and know-how the book market, organization and research, finding new markets, interviewing, humor, agents, writer's fatigue and more. 317 pp. $10.95.

Writing and Selling Science Fiction, compiled by the Science Fiction Writers of America. A comprehensive handbook to an exciting but oft-misunderstood genre. Eleven articles by top-flight sf writers on markets, characters, dialog, "crazy" ideas, world-building, alien-building, money and more. 197 pp. $8.95.

Writing for Children and Teen-agers, by Lee Wyndham. Author of over 50 children's books shares her secrets for selling to this large, lucrative market. Features: the 12-point recipe for plotting, and the Ten Commandments for Writers. 253 pp. $9.95.

Writing Popular Fiction, by Dean R. Koontz. How to write mysteries, suspense, thrillers, science fiction, Gothic romances, adult fantasy, Westerns and erotica. Here's an inside guide to lively fiction, by a lively novelist. 232 pp. $8.95.

Writing the Novel: From Plot to Print, by Lawrence Block. Practical advice on how to write any kind of novel. 256 pp. $10.95.

(1-2 books, add $1.00 postage and handling; 3 or more, additional 25¢ each. Allow 30 days for delivery. Prices subject to change without notice.)
Writer's Digest Books, Dept. B, 9933 Alliance Road, Cincinnati, Ohio 45242